777 Reviv

This little book stem from notes that my wife, Esther, fondly called Essie and myself made over several years whilst studying the precious Word of God. We both knew Jesus as our savior since childhood. We realized that Christ is Lord and had many opportunities to witness how Jesus is the leader of our household. When she went to Jesus, I was struck with what first seemed as devastation. I miss her so much…

But God!

Jesus stood by me and my daughters, Jonandi and Mariska. My grandchildren miss out on the love and fellowship that only a grandmother could give. It is with praise to our Savior that we offer this study of our old memories how Jesus walked with us in the study of His Word.

*** I Hereby declare God's glory among the heathen; His wonders among all people; for the Lord is great and greatly to be praised. He is to be feared above all gods.
His works are marvelous.
Nobody will drive me out from abiding in the inheritance of the Lord.

*** Declare God's glory as even the heavens declare the glory of God and the firmament shows His handy work.
Declare His glory among the heathen, His wonders among all people.
The Lord is great and greatly to be praised. He is to be feared above all gods and idols, as the gods of the nations are vanities, emptiness and things of naught.

*** Declare God's righteousness as the heavens show His glory to all people.

REVIVED IN CHRIST.

Index

Index

To Them That Claim: IT IS All A LIE ...

Did you not hear...? There is not a morsel of truth in the total
story. All the time I thought that there was a God, and now this.
It's silly even to sit and type with my two fingers? For what! Tears
gush from my inner most. You said you would come and now this.
Here I am trapped in the ambush. I feel alone against the enemy.
Not a soul around. You promised that you would never forsake me,
but what is this all about?   I spent my whole life seeking shelter,
surging for a fleck of food, gathering newspapers for heat and a
bed and looking for a God that in a time like this just did not show
up. Every year this time there are lights and trees full of stuff of all
sorts of decorations. Songs are repeating words of happy holidays,
but what is so happy when all people dash around spending and
spending and spending. And God seems to be a silly doll in a box
of straw, Wow, and I am still a slave of loneliness and
hunger....and all the little children like me.   Yes, those bruised,
tired weary children sold for misuse...They are still abused and
trotted on by sexual perverts. Hear my sole screaming out in
anguish! The gloom of reality, brothel forth on tender flesh of
children as money jingle bells the tills...

  Jesus is all about you loving children lies, or what? Holy Spirit
could some authority with sense stand up firmer than just
legislation on paper...?   How many more precious children must
sleep on streets, city streets scratching trash for semi rotten bits of
disease filled food?

My God, My God why have you forsaken me?   Is that the cry of
the silent tear from this precious little homeless kid? Yet I know
God loves children. You must be mistaken, you proclaim, as
another child dies prematurely ... and Jesus is waiting on your
answer. Are you the answer?

  May be that shoulder shrug was just a muscle contraction? May
be you could check the park tonight and listen for a small voice
crying. You might even become the hand of God helping....

2   Are You Ready For Christmas?

<u>Dear Jesus:</u>

I was asked this question but I could not really answer. I wish to speak with you to hear your teachings. How do you answer a question like that?   Little child of Bethlehem, you are just a newborn baby and nobody knows your birth weight. Nobody told us the color of your eyes. Did you have a touch of cramps after Mary gave you your first feed? Precious child, you came from the protective heart of Abba who so dearly loved the entire world of people even me and all of us. God sent His best, His only, His all, that part of His Father's heart that swells because of You, His only begotten Son.

Listen to what Abba speaks of you little babe: When the time came for me to show you favor: I HEARD YOU... When the day arrived for me to save You, I helped you. Your little hands are so beautiful, and those eyes are heavenly, proclaiming the hour to receive the favor of God. You really just cuddled yourself snugly into my heart. It feels as if you want to live there forever! Please stay in my heart. This is the day to be saved.... You are a KING, You know, and so lovable. I do not understand why you would be on offer for the sin of all the people. So special! So beautiful! Why must you be a peace offering? Palpitations rush my heart as I think about this world that you came into. It is just hate anger and retaliation. O how distasteful and rotten. Still you came to my rescue. God really loved us in this world so much to give you, little baby. A baby destined to be that Man of sorrows. Just how could you grow up with the thought of it all? Even to carry only my bags of sin makes you my hero! I cuddle the little lamb as tears show my deep love for Jesus. Thank you for that little smile on your face... which will be mutilated by the blood of your sacrifice for my sins.

Thank You for stretching your little hand towards me, touching me as I weep. I lack words to describe even thinking of blood coming from your pierced little cuddling hands... Jesus my Lord, O how faithfully you watch my every move. My faith is preciously strengthened. I believe in this young Baby.

He comes from eternity, born to conquer the sin of all human beings? How human and O so Godly. Thank You Abba for this offering that you suffered for us. Jesus is the eternal offer to reconcile Abba to us. Thank you for His mother that kept all these things in her precious heart. Even the Holy Spirit made that 'thing' called our Redeemer.

Am I ready for your coming again? I am, I believe, I received your special gift of salvation. You are my sanctuary. You took my sins, and made me a baby whom you spared from the wages of sin. You made my darkness midday light. I was far away. You pulled me into your everlasting love. I can now race towards the finishing line, even as my blood is pumping joy through my arteries. Faith shields me by your blood and in yourself. Christ Himself prepared me for Christmas. Christ is my Christmas and it does not matter what else anyone say about that fact.

3   MICH –TAM

WE are coming into THY presence even with words of praises and
thanksgiving O Lord. Thou art the Eternal God Almighty. Let us
contemplate and meditate the pages of Thy Word, even the fullness
of the Book of life. Every dot and title is placed in absolute perfect
harmony with Your Being. What joy to experience your greatness
and majesty! It is pleasant to my sole to behold that which is
written in the pages of your Word. It speaks loud, and then at times
with whispers of such tender love. Beautiful and uplifting! My
heart adores you. You loved me first! It is no secret! You first
covered me in eternal Love.
  Please haste not, speak on, and overflow my soul with streams of
living waters, even fountains of everlasting joy, soaking my being
with the filling of eternity. Oh so precious. I dare neither to speak
nor breathe in the presence and majesty of your eternal Being. This
is fullness of peace and glory....Your Words are purer than silver
tried in an earthen furnace and purified seven times. As you open
my eyes, that splendor of what is written of Thee, the fullness of
The Book, graciously flow up and I do behold.... Jesus.
You captivate my gaze and all that I can see is You, permeating
through every syllabus and phrase on every page. I become the
slave of the greatness that you are and who you are even the Name
above all names! Softly I whisper Jesus, and that Name grows and
multiplies until I could hear nothing else but the sounds of the
heavenly host worshipping; Jesus God Almighty. The whole earth
proclaims the glory of God. The Lord is in His Holy temple: hush!
Be still! Lo! I cannot else but pray and surrender completely as I
put my trust in Thee. Thou art my portion of my inheritance. My
cup runs over. Thou maintain my lot. I have set the Lord always
before me. Because He is at my right hand, I shall not be moved.
My heart is glad and my flesh rest in hope. I am still and behold
the path of life. The gate is straight and the way is narrow but, that
I follow. This Pathway of Life leads to eternal life.
I desire to be one that finds the way, the truth and the life. In
obedience to God is wisdom even to do the will of the Father.

Come let us be still and hear the sayings of Jesus. Let us be wise and also do those sayings. Be still my soul and believe because even though the rains will descend, the floods may come, the winds may blow, and the house may be beaten upon. Because my house is founded on the rock called Jesus, this house will not fall. I sigh of relief, joy, and astonishment. The doctrine and teaching of Jesus is pure wisdom followed by signs and wonders of conformation of His mighty works. Now I ponder upon the wisdom of the Lord. Holy Spirit teaches us in all wisdom. It is Holy Spirit that anointed Jesus and us including me, so that we can share the gospel to all. Like Jesus we should also receive Holy Spirit. We should stand before the throne of God Almighty on a daily basis to be anointed for the task to spread the gospel and to heal the broken hearted. Like Jesus we should set the captives free, heal the blind and set at liberty them that are oppressed. That is why my Lord came and died on the cross. Now be still before the only God of eternity and decide if we can afford not to be obedient to the call to spread the gospel. It is the will of God that we should go out and tell.

Bare His witness. As many as received Him, He gave the power to become the sons of God.

It takes faith. Believe on His Name and you will be born again. It is not of the will of man nor by the flesh, but by Holy Spirit. The man of sorrows, Jesus, had no splendor or stately form. A completely human man acquainted with grief. He was bruised by God for He was made an offering for sin… To think it was for my sins that He poured out His life and suffered unto death. Be informed, the death by crucifixion is a brutally cruel way to die. He bares the death of the cross for the sins of all, and made intercession for all transgressors. We have to accept His offer of the grace of God. No matter what happens, I declare;

Although the fig tree shall not blossom, neither shall fruit be in the vines, the labor of the olive shall fail, and the field shall yield no meat, the flock shall be cut off from the fold and there shall be no herd in the stalls,

* YET, I WILL REJOICE IN THE LORD. * I WILL JOY IN THE GOD OF MY SALVATION. *HE IS THE SON OF GOD AND THUS ETERNALLY GOD* COME LET US WALK IN HIGH PLACES EVEN BEFORE GOD AND HIS THRONE….
* BECAUSE I AM WASHED IN THE BLOOD OF THE LAMB,
* I AM PURCHASED BY THE LORD FOR A PRICE…

* I CAN BE STILL AND REST IN MY SOUL,
*FOR I AM A CHILD OF GOD.
* I AM JUSTIFIED, I AM REDEEMED, AND MY SINS ARE
ALL FORGIVEN.
* THERE IS NO MORE CONDEMNATION FOR MY SINS.
* I CANNOT BE SEPERATED FROM GOD AS I CAN
APPROACH THE LORD IN PRAYER WITH FREEDOM AND
CONFIDENCE.
*PRAISE AND HONOUR BE UNTO JESUS AND THE
FATHER THROUGH THE HOLY SPIRIT!!
*WHAT A GLORIOUS PLAN OF SALVATION.

4   The Humbleness of King Jesus.

'God if you are there here my call….?' I waited ….   'I am on my
own.' Still there was silence. ''I feel so down and flat on my face. I
know that it has been so long since I even tried to speak with you
or come near to you. It was easy when my mom prayed for us. But
she really freaked me out at times. I slipped and am in a lot of
trash. I don't think I can get out of my troubles. I tried but just get
deeper in. It helps me nothing. My career, future and dreams are
shattered. I know now that I do need your help… I lost everything,
my house, vehicle, my office, and my income. Somehow I lost
friends and even my dignity…'
'Are you talking to me?'
  The gush of words from my lips was interrupted. I looked around
but saw nobody. Silence followed.
I thought that was strange. I could still see nobody but offered
another attempt: 'Where are you?'
Softly HE spoke and said: 'whosoever will be chief among you, let
him be the servant amongst you.'
Shame came over me as I always wanted things my way. I serve
no body.
Again I heard His gentle voice: 'Let me finish my sentence as you
do not know how to listen.''
My ways flash before me and I had to admit that is the truth: Yes
Lord, I am sorry…
There was silence as I waited. And after a while that felt very
prolonged…, Jesus said: I came not to be the chief: the Son of man
came not to be ministered unto but to serve, and to give His life a
ransom for many.
That felt like as if He knows everything... I dared: Have mercy on
me O Lord, Thou son of David.
In faith I heard the Lord answer: What will ye that I shall do unto
you? It struck me that Jesus offered hands on help.
In deep respect I asked: Lord that you open my eyes and speak to
my heart. Jesus had compassion on me and touched my eyes.

Immediately I received insight and my heart was burning in me. I decided to follow Jesus.

Thou shall love the Lord thy God with all thy heart and with all thy sole and with thy entire mind.

As I thought for a moment, it dawned upon me: I loved myself more than I loved Jesus. His sharp double edged sword pierced right to the core. I loved myself first. My head became heavy as I could not keep it up in His righteous presence and I knew the answer is to pray for the love of God to become my prime motive and desire.

I asked: 'Jesus, would you please give me eternal love toward you? Change my heart'. I sighed, Love of God cover me. Living waters make eternal waves towards me and my neighbors.'

Then Jesus said the most precious words I ever understood. ''I FIRST LOVED YOU EVEN IN YOUR MOTHERS WOMB. I love you eternally and made sure that you could be with me forever.''

Amazing! GRACE.

The reality of His love was transferred into my heart and soul and understanding. I realized the Word spells it out so clearly: God is love. LOVE is His special gift. It is greater than any gift. God commended his love for me even while I was still a sinner. God loved the world so much that he gave Jesus, His only begotten Son….God sent His only begotten Son that we might live through Him. O Lord this is what you are offering: LIFE. You are offering the propitiation for our sins. Your love is perfected in us.

The face of Jesus shined of love and I melted. To know the love of Jesus Christ passes knowledge. Just to think that ye might be filled with all the benefits of God! My Lord smiled.

''He that hath my commandments and keep them, he it is that loves Me and he that loves Me, shall be loved by the Father and I will love him and will manifest myself to him.''

5   <u>Love One another</u>

Then He continued: Thou should love thy neighbor. This is MY
COMMANDMENT, that ye love one another as I have loved you.
That is an order…. Love like Jesus? Wow!
Greater love has no man than this; that a man lay down his life for
friends. Now that loves!
These things I command you, that ye love one another.''
'' I love you and you love me, we are a happy family. '' The song
of my childhood sounds through my mind.
By now I realized perfectly well that I must, on order, love my
neighbor and the prayer came; The Lord teaches me to be humble
and loving and ready for when he comes again as the King of
kings.
Make me give up myself entirely. Make me an empty vessel to
receive the power of the Holy Spirit to live, dwell and work in me
every day. Fill me with your light, love and yourself to the fullest
of my capacity.
Jesus looked upon me as He looked upon Peter. Even as Peter
broke because of him denying Jesus three times, I knew that my
selfishness and self-righteousness exceeded all that.
I wept before Jesus and somehow I recalled how Jesus wept for
His friend, Lazarus…. I cried even more as His grace toward me
included me as a friend. I am a friend of Jesus. Tears of
thankfulness made me feel so humble to think the King Himself
consider me His friend.
….And Jesus asked me: Do you love me? Yes Lord I do. Again he
asked: Do you love me?
Three times He asked and again I broke out in tears before the
Almighty God because I know that that is also the reason why you
read this. Do you love Jesus? So I let go of pride because I rather
have Jesus. Then the humble Holy Spirit who gives all for Jesus,
asked me to come and stay within me. Gladly Holy Spirit, come

and abide within me and teach me your ways. Help me despite my
weakness. Help me to do your will. Let me walk in your presence
and enter boldly into the throne room of God Almighty.
Abide with me; yes abide in me….as I abide in Thee.
Grant me a place in your Holy presence. I walk and talk in the
presence of him that forms the mountains and created the wind.
Lord, you declare unto man your thoughts and create the morning
darkness. You tread upon the high places of the earth; the LORD,
THE GOD OF HOSTS IS YOUR NAME.
I prepare to meet my GOD.., but where shall we meet?   Then the
Lord answered; Come behind the veil. Come to the real throne of
grace. Enter boldly. Spend time here with Me. Start even now.
Come in by the blood and seek God that made the seven stars and
the Orion. I turned the shadow of death into the morning.
God made the day dark with night when Jesus died for you on the
cross. I call the waters of the sea and pour them out upon the face
of the earth. The Lord is My Name. Seek God and not evil.
Lord I hear your voice. Lovely are your dwellings. My soul longs
and faints for Thy courts. My heart and flesh cry out for the Living
God. Blessed are they that dwell in Thy house. A day in Thy courts
is better than a thousand… Please teach me more about you. Then
the Lord answered: Come and enter into the secret place with Me.
Come and receive my glory and see my face. Come let us talk.
Come by My Spirit and be changed from glory to glory. I will
speak from my most Holy place and fill you. Come here were the
ground is Holy. It is your secret place where we meet personally.
Come in. Come up here…BE in awe of the most High place. Sit on
My lap my child with me on the throne of gold. Sit under the
wings of my cherubs. Join me at the mercy seat and receive grace
and favor. There you will receive power and authority. Listen to
the testimony of miracles as we develop our intimate relationship.
Take up boldness and people would know by your testimony that
you have been with me even by your eloquence of speech. Come
let me show you the way that you should go in confidence.
Wisdom is given here. See Jesus on my right hand, high and lifted
up. Come and ask from me. My robe fills the temple and the angels
sing Holy, Holy, Holy is the Lord of Hosts. Come and breathe in
my Holy air… Let not your heart be troubled. I am preparing your
place.
There is a forerunner for us preparing the way, Jesus our High
Priest. In faith I join and sing with Moses: Let me dwell in the

secret place of the most high. Let me abide under the shadow of the Almighty, my refuge and fortress, my God in whom I trust. What trouble can attack me, O that I may dwell in the House of the Lord Jesus?

6   LOVE YOUR NEIGHBOUR AS YOURSELF

Jesus tells me, no, rather teach me how to love. As I ask this of You Lord Jesus, I feel unable to even attempt. It is such a vastly acclaimed topic whom so many sang about before. I hear about love that is to help someone in need and as I watch on television and listen to the media, I seem to understand. We can have such compassion that urges a heartfelt force of action. Others see and respond and react by sharing compassionate money complying with your standard of love. Was love penetrating all dimensions and borders in the mighty name of Jesus?   What is love Lord? 'He that loves not knows not God.'
Jesus, I still stumble, even on this question? '' How do I see love in a child sold to slavery in a sex industry?
Why would a parent sell his child? Why do men or ladies sell themselves to brothels?
Then softly Jesus answered… That is not love! I shall teach you even as you are surging my Word.
THOUGH I speak with the tongues of men and angels and have not charity, I am become as sounding brass, or a tinkling cymbal. What do you mean by that Lord?
Jesus spoke to my heart:' Pride serves not love.'
It is not that simple, but to you I give this understanding: amongst my children who are called by my Name I find pride. However after prayer and supplication they ask to have my forgiveness, then I always do and my special blessings are for them that believe. I grant them that gift to speak in different tongues, even their heavenly language. I bless them in the Holy Spirit and their heavenly tongue. It is a free gift. My Spirit prays in earnest understanding of their needs and the benefit of the Kingdom of My Father. This is unto the glory of the Father, the Son and the Holy Spirit. Speaking in the tongue of the Spirit of God is also unto the

answering of the prayer to the benefit of my child who received the tongue of the Holy Spirit.

Praise and worship me in your special heavenly tongue. Do that in my Spirit. Rejoice then and be thankful. Be build up in your spirit and understanding and preparation to witness my gospel to the entire world. I am preparing you for this great commission of sharing God's love to your neighbors.

There are other gifts that I give freely to my children: the gift of Prophecy, Wisdom, Understand all mysteries, and all Knowledge of the Word of God. The gift of all Faith even to remove mountains:

But note, without charity you are nothing. I thought softly in amazing wonder at the understanding all mysteries or even all knowledge. Jesus gently pressed on: You can go on to bestow all your goods to feed the poor, and give your body to be burned, but have not charity, it profits me nothing!

This slowly penetrated my thick skull, charity benefits me and my Jesus and all to whom HE BENEFITS WITH THE CHARITY. O that I could love from the depth of my heart. Jesus said these words show the nature of Charity. Make these your very own character:

Charity suffers long, is kind, and does not envy.

Charity does not display success or possessions boastfully.

Charity is not puffed up, or behaves not itself unseemly. Charity seeks not her own, and is *not easily provoked.*

Charity thinks no evil, rejoices not in iniquity, but rejoices in the truth.

Charity bears all things, believes all things, hopes all things, and endures all things.

CHARITY NEVER FAILS.

Suddenly I realized that I failed God's description of His love and charity. Lord I lack charity. I need your way to love.

NOW ABIDES FAITH, HOPE, and CHARITY. THESE THREE ...BUT THE GREATEST OF THESE IS CHARITY.

Again Jesus softly spoke: Organize to help those in need, give help, give money or food to those in need, give help and kindness to people and you will understand and live some of MY LOVE.

7   <u>WHAT THEN IS A CHRISTIAN?</u>

This is a difficult question but seems so easy at first thought, as for instance: ''Is a Christian somebody that believes in Christ and follow's Him?'' I would argue that this definition has some truth in it, but even just the Name ''Christ '' or Messiah, is vastly untouched by this simplistic point of view, and the 'Name above all names' is not included. The power and miraculous facts are not even vaguely represented. For that reason I have decided to relate more to the character of Christ Jesus that the follower of this King of kings can identify with. Ask Christ prayerfully to exemplify more accurately in your own lives as I ask Him to show me what it takes to be a child of God, a brother of Christ, in whom the Holy Spirit of God rules, and reigns. The effect would be that we, by the grace of God who is love, would grow in the semblance of our Master ....

How do you follow the Christ? Which one are you talking about? Do not think I am just playing with words. In this dissertation I must state that I am referring to the Jewish born, son of Mary, conceived in a miraculous way, as the Holy Spirit came over her. This 'thing' that was born was called Jesus, the Son of the Almighty God, who thus became a new being also called the Son of Man. This is the true Christ, Jesus the everlasting God that sits on the right hand of the throne of God Almighty. Jesus who will come again soon, is God the Son. Is this the person, God, you serve?   Are you a Christian just because you think you are? Thinking like that does not cut it. I might think I am the smartest, most intelligent male on earth, but a few simple tests may expose my folly. Your everlasting eternal life is worth much more than speculation about, or assumption of any fact. It is the Gospel Truth as found in the Holy Bible that sets you free from condemnation, and secures your eternal destination.

Some say a Christian is anyone that is born again. Even there are problems, as the word of God requires that we should hear the voice of God and follow and do the will of God. Moreover it seems that we should also be known by God. He wants to know you as His child. He wants to meet you in your prayers and sup with you. Please seek personal relationship with God. It is priceless to Him even as He desires your presence and devotions. He longs to hear your sighs of love and compassion for Him. He wants to meet up with you in the holiest of holy place in the throne room of Heaven. God loves you.   He will accept you only via the greatest cleaning process whereby you are cleaned and washed in the blood of Jesus and reconciled with Him. That took the blood of His only begotten Son. That took the cross of Golgotha outside the camp were the scapegoat became Jesus, and the hanging on the cross the curse. The death and blood and tasting of death and experiencing of hell, became salvation's offer even as JESUS CONQUERED IT ALL...

Surely a Christian becomes saved if this offer becomes his most precious treasure ever, even as he receives new birth in Christ and no longer lives by this world. The Christian dies to this world! The world's pleasures are left behind. He lives for Christ. The Spirit of God lives in Him and introduces him to the Trinity: FATHER, SON AND HOLY SPIRIT. Now the Holy Spirit teaches you and me the way to follow, in order to become God's cuddled child, well known and loved by the God of love. I call Him Abba. Precious, O such a precious Father! Should you proclaim this! Are you serious! Who would not jump of joy! Proclaim the gift of Salvation to all! Rejoice, sing, dance, make merry in manifold ways! Jesus is alive and because of that I can face tomorrow and all adversaries. Follow the teachings about Jesus. It is written in the entire volume of the Bible book from Genesis to Revelation. It is fresh every day as new revelations daily exude out of the Book and into your being. Read it. Blessed is the Healer of my sole. This is the way pointed out to you. Get a running! Run the race! Move it! Study the Bible and be shown a worthy student... Let your life manifest the qualities of Jesus. That is the witness of Christ in You! Complete the race. Win the race. Receive the crown!

8 God Wants To Know You

What is God looking for when it comes to you? Do you know His criteria to live victoriously? The meaning of the Greek word for a Christian is the ''anointed one. '' God has anointed thee with the oil of gladness above thy fellows. The Spirit of God is upon me, because the Lord has anointed me to preach good tidings unto the meek...to bind up the broken hearted, to proclaim liberty to the captives, and to set them free. There are people who may live according to the principles and teachings of Christianity, but who are not children of God. Think about the challenges that each of these would be. During the Roman Empire, a Christian was called 'a Christ like one' and many lives were lost during the persecution of those days. Christians of the times of persecution were proud to be called 'Christ like.' Many Christians die currently because they are not prepared to deny their faith. Persecution of churches and Christians are daily occurrences. I would urge the people that believe and would be prepared to suffer unto death for Christ to:
*Have fellowship with the Father on a daily basis.
*The Lord's joy is your strength. *Spend time with the Lord.
*Seek the Lord and His strength. * Share the little pleasures of daily living with your best friend, God is he...
*Give yourself in loving obedience to God who shall renew your strength. *Desire to worship God and so do with all you have.
*Love God with all your strength.
*Know how deeply Christ Jesus loves us, and be full of joy.
*Draw close to and love our pears, as loving brothers and sisters of

and in Christ. *Submit your free will unto the Holy Spirit. *Even if I am weak, my strength is made perfect in Christ. *Live a Holy life by doing what the Spirit of God tells you today.
*Do not wait for tomorrow to do that.
*Be still and know that I am God.
*Know the Lord by His Word.
*God knows us by our fruits.
*We know that God is truth and that truth will set us free. *Be aware as there is but one God.
*As for me I KNOW whom I have believed.
*God knows our hearts and all things about us;
* Our foolishness. * My thoughts. * The way of the righteous. * The days of the upright.
  The Lord knows the secrets of our hearts and our thoughts.
* The Lord knows our frame and what things we need.
* The Lord knows them that are His.
* God knows all things.
*God wants you to know that He is not far away. He lives in our hearts.
* You can turn to Him any moment. In fact He desires to speak with His children.
*Speak up now.
*He listens.

9   THE PEACE OF BIRTH OF CHRIST

The birth of a prince is associated with celebrations. Even so do we celebrate the birth of my Lord JESUS as He is the Prince of Peace? The time of this season is a time of peace so profound that the angels of heaven proclaimed the arrival of baby Jesus. God the Father send His only begotten Son to this world. Should we not stop, look up and reflect what it means to get SUCH an offering of peace on earth. Take a break and reflect what God is doing for you. He offers peace to you. I think it would be good to come nearer to sit down. THE AMAZING GOD knows you by name. He counted every hair on your head. He created you. The Lord leads you by the way you should go. He teaches you to profit. Listen to HIS commandments as it brings peace like a river, and righteousness as the waves of the sea. Come here and join the angels sing the glory of God in the highest as He gives peace on earth and goodwill toward man. Even His goodwill is so glorious that our words cannot describe it. Walk the path of the shepherds who went up from the field to find Mary and the child called Jesus. Find Jesus there… Once you found Jesus make sure that you find the Holy Spirit, the Comforter, who in tender love would explain that our Father in heaven sent the Holy Ghost in the Name of Jesus to teach you all things about Jesus and bring all things about Jesus to your remembrance and understanding. Jesus leaves His peace with us as His present toward us so that our hearts need not to trouble, nor to be afraid.   We experience the peace of God even if all seemed to have failed. The peace that Jesus leaves you are not like this world gives, but rather it is in Jesus that we have peace. BE IN JESUS."

He covers you in love. Though your beloved died, or the crop failed, though you now have diabetes or cancer, remember that we will have tribulation in this world, but cheer up as Jesus overcame this world and so can we. If we have faith in Jesus we will also have peace with GOD. Thus be justified in your faith in JESUS, and have peace with God. Stand in faith, grace, and rejoice in the hope of the glory of God.

Jesus is our peace and reconciliation with God. Now we rejoice in the hope of the glory of GOD. We have access by faith and grace into the glory of God. ALSO now we have the peace of God which passes all understanding. If you are born in Christ, your birthright is Peace in HIM. God makes you perfect in every good work to do His will. This all is by the New Everlasting Covenant of that Great Shepherd, so that your work would be pleasing in the sight of GOD.

FOR UNTO US A CHILD IS BORN WHO GIVES PEACE. THERE IS NO END OF THE FAVOUR AND GRACE OF GOD. THIS WONDERFUL COUNSELOR, THE MIGHTY GOD, THE EVERLASTING FATHER REIGHNS ETERNALLY. THERE IS THE PRINCE OF PEACE ON DAVIDS THRONE. MAKE HIM RULER IN OUR HEARTS. HIS KINGDOM WILL BE ESTABLISHED AND UPHELD IN JUSTICE, RIGHTEOUSNESS AND PEACE FOR EVER. THE ZEAL OF THE LORD ALMIGHTY ACCOMPLISHES THIS. WORSHIP THE BABE WHO IS THE LAMB OF GOD AND WE SHALL SEE JESUS GLORIFIED!!

10   Then There Was Charlotte...Who Thought...

If God loved me He would not have treated me this way;
*my health is shattered. *day by day I struggle. *I have no friends,
or at least no true friends. *money is not a problem, I simply have
none. *Whatever I try, simply fails.
*my old car, the only one I have, just blew its machine. *my
children suffer from that generation gap. *nobody loves me except
my dog and he is ill. *my husband died and I have to speak up if I
want to hear any human voice in my house. *that was my second
husband, the first one abused me. *the taxman is selling my house
on auction. *I really lose my temper because God, if He even
exists, surely is crushing me all over......and by the way, *all my
wounds get septic.
STOP!!!
Do you really feel that way? Are you tired of yourself? Why do
you persist in clinging to your anger, or even hatred? Have you
nothing or no one else to lean on?
There is someone that I know who said to me that the one who
comes to Him; He will by no means cast out.
That is Jesus speaking. He is the Son of God. He is not making a
big fuss about who you are, or how smart or great you should be,
He simply invites you to talk to Him and tell Him all about your
problems. Come just as you are. He knows already about all the
hard times and all the problems you have mentioned and even
those that you did not tell anybody yet....He offers his help for

free, actually the price has already been paid on your behalf. Is that not sounding like unwarranted grace? Actually He says to all that labor and are heavily laden just like you, that He will give you an all-round brake so that you could surely get a rest. Jesus will not cast you out but would rather treat you better than the best husband could ever even dream of. Can you here with your heart His soft gentle voice calling? He will not cast you out. He paid a most expensive price concerning your troubles and will lead you out of this darkness into a new life. If He takes a job on, He does it absolutely perfectly.

Now remember those things that I have revealed to you belong to you, but also to your children. If you accept Him, you are justified because his blood was shed for your sins. Would you say to Him, also called the ''Lamb of God'' that you come. Why not right now? Get all of those blemishes off your memory, your soul and even your heart as they break you in pieces by even remembering. Jesus will help to do that, actually He would ask even God the Father to remember His promise to remove your sins and iniquities as far as the east is from the west.

Your spots may have been like scarlet, but you will become as white as snow. Common now, do not fear little flock because if you step out, you would find that it pleases God the Father to make you part of His kingdom. The emergency number to heaven is called: 'O Lamb of God I come.' It does not mind if you feel or are poor, wretched, or blind just whisper: ''Lord I come''. All you need you will find in HIM even healing your heart and riches untold. God will receive you and welcome you heartily. You will be cleansed and so relieved that you will rejoice: O LAMB OF GOD I COME.

By the way here is some gift for you to stand moment by moment in.

Claim:
*I am a new person. *I have grown together with Christ in His death and resurrection. *I am dead for sins but alive in Christ to serve God. *I am in Christ and He is in me via the Holy Spirit who lives in me and teaches me. *Jesus fills my soul with the resurrected life of Himself. *Christ is now my life by faith.
The effect of all this is that my old self died with Christ on the cross.
I now live for and in Christ for the rest of my life here on earth and

have eternal life following as my certainty …
WOW! The inhabitants of heaven rejoice for Charlotte thought, searched and found the MOST PRECIOUS pearl and His Name Is Jesus…….

11   GABATTA; WHAT IS TRUTH?

When Pilate had to judge Jesus, he found himself asking the Accused:'' What is truth?''
Did he realize that the Eternal Witness of the Truth was standing in front of him…?   One wonders?
God is truth. He who blesses himself in the earth shall bless himself in the God of truth.
Jesus came to earth not to destroy the law, or the prophets, but to fulfil. Till heaven and earth pass, one jot or one title shall in no wise pass from the law, till all be fulfilled. Do the law that the Holy Spirit has put into the tablets of your heart and teach them, for that is honor and greatness in the Kingdom of heaven. Listen to the law that the Holy Spirit write in our minds. Obey the law of love of Jesus. Jesus came to minister, and give His life a ransom for many….
How does Jesus fulfil the truth? God is truth. The Holy Spirit cannot lie. Neither can Jesus lie.
JESUS came as Redeemer and paid the price;
*To save from death all who have sinned as said in Hos13:14: I will ransom them from the power of the grave, I will redeem them from death…. 1Cor15:52; …the dead shall be raised incorruptible.

*To save us from sickness: Our bodies are the temple of the Holy Spirit and our flesh shall be fresher than a child's.

*To save us from sin: The Son of man came…to give His life as a ransom for many…..In whom we have redemption through His blood, the forgiveness of sins, according to the riches of His grace.

*To save us from the enemy by the arm of the Lord….who gave Himself a ransom for all.

He is our Witness to the people, our Leader and Commander. Jesus is given to us. He has glorified us.

*Whilst He is to be found, let us seek Him. Call on His Name while He is near.

Please hear God's plea!

*Let the wicket forsake his way, and the unrighteous man his thoughts, and let him return unto the Lord.

*God will have mercy upon Him for He will abundantly pardon.

*Jesus is given to forgive and is the only way to God.

*God is faithful and would not suffer you to be tempted above that you are able, but will with temptation also make a way to escape that ye may be able to bear it.

*Make up your mind and resist the temptation.

*Continue in the Word as then we are Jesus' disciples indeed and we shall know the truth.

*The Truth about Jesus will set you free.

12   THE SPIRIT OF TRUTH

The Spirit of Truth is come. He will guide you into all truth; for He shall not speak of Himself, but whatsoever He shall hear, that shall He speak; and He shall show you things to come. That speaks of our beloved Holy Spirit. Come o Holy Spirit; teach me the truth about Jesus.

*Jesus shows us the way to be born again: He said: Except a man is born again, he cannot see the Kingdom of God.

Except a man be born of water and of Spirit, he cannot enter into the Kingdom of God. Water is used as the figure of our salvation. Jesus claims that whosoever drinks of the water that He shall give him, shall never thirst, but the water that Jesus shall give him, shall be in him a well of water, springing up into everlasting life.

The Holy Spirit in us makes to draw water out of the wells of salvation, so that we shall say;

Praise the Lord, call upon his Name, declare his doings among the people, make mention that His Name is exalted. Sing unto the Lord; for He has done excellent things. God gave the ordinance of the sun to give light by day, the moon and stars by night. He divided the see and decreed that it should never cover the earth. He made the ordinances of the sun, moon and stars to be eternal and the heavens infinity. The unsearchableness of the earth is His doing. He declared the eternity of Israel's union with Jehovah. Make this known in all the earth!

O the flock of Jesus, His sheep, hears the voice of Jesus, hears the voice of God as the Holy Spirit speaks and direct us, walking before us to show the way.

Jesus is the way and as we see Jesus, we see the Father. God Triune is one, knows us intimately because of the reconciliation, and will never leave or forsake us now and forever. That child who accepts this, God will not disown now, or throughout eternity. Child of God forever.

Access to God's throne is mine to speak, and to pray in worship and adoration.

I am His as I have been given life by the Spirit. It is the Holy Spirit that quickens my spirit and body.

He also quickens you who believe. Come then into the courts of heaven. Sing hallelujah.

The words Jesus speak unto us, they are Spirit! They are life now and even eternal life! Live in the Holy Spirit every moment. Read the word of God. It is alive.

The Holy Spirit in me and you will raise us up for eternal life, as He did raise Jesus up, from the death of the cross. The same Spirit lives in me! That I believe. We will be raised up incorruptible because of the victory on the cross. Wow! Jesus is truly the way, the truth and the life.

So Father I am come unto Thee by the truth of Jesus, Who said that if I know Jesus, I know the Father. Glory! I know the Father and He knows me! Nothing can separate us.

The very Spirit of God Himself teaches me the truth right from my inner most being.

The Holy Spirit is known to me as He declared Himself to be in me and I surely accept that with my heart, body and soul. This power that you read is the impartation of the Spirit of God in me even as He comforts me and helps me to understand. Praise the Godly Teacher who shows me the fullness of truth as I study under His guidance.

13   Glorify Jesus through Holy Spirit

No one can reveal the truth of Christ our Savior, and help me to
glorify Him as His Spirit Himself.
The Holy Spirit reveals events and how to be a witness of Christ as
He cheers me and you on. He is the Chief Witness of Christ.
The Holy Spirit is He that convinced me of my sin, requiring the
judgment of God and showed me the path of redemption and
righteousness.
We are no longer of this world. We have the Word of God.
Jesus intercedes for us and prays that we should be kept from evil
and should be kept by God for His sacred purpose... He stands in,
as we consecrate ourselves wholly to God and His service.
We should separate ourselves to be sanctified through the truth, to
be one in God the Father, the Holy Spirit, and Jesus the Christ.
We do not glorify ourselves, but receive glory in Christ.
We are sanctified and sent into the world to tell about Jesus.
He desires truth in our inward parts and He gives wisdom to me to
know His Word even by my study into His Word.
As I open my lips, my mouth shall especially show forth the

praises of the Lord.

I am covered with the feathers of God and under His Almighty wings. I shall trust His truth, my shield and buckler. It is so cozy here as God grants us tender loving care and protection from the arrows of the enemy.

The Word was made flesh. Jesus is the incarnation of the Word of God, and dwelt among us.

We beheld the glory, of the only begotten Son of God the Father, full of grace and truth. Truly, He is the only begotten Son of God! On the earth the Son of God also became the son of man, who is fully human. Completely one and living the life of a human so that He could as a human understand and take up all our sins upon Him.

He brought grace, the Grace of God.

He had one focus before Him: redemption of the World.

In the process of our redemption we are made perfect. Once we accepted Jesus, his eternal gift of salvation, completed on the cross, transforms our lives and we shine like eternal stars. Our change over from evil to good takes up our body mind and soul. It is unquestionable that this person now serves the purposes of God's eternal kingdom. Jesus does not have to repeat the cross and His sacrifice ever again. We can be saved. I am reconciled with Almighty God.

God cannot tolerate any sin in His perfect presence, being, or heaven, as the wages of sin is death. The wages of Sin is eternal condemnation in hell. After the deed on the cross, God sees only what Jesus has done. By His suffering Jesus took all our punishment as required. He conquered death hell and the grave. By His Stripes I Am Saved. So we speak the truth in Love, and in love grow up unto Jesus in all things. He is the Head, and we are the body. He shows us the blue print to guide our lives on the earth. The call is to study Him in His Book to perfectly show our self, approved not unto men, but unto God as a workman that needs not to be ashamed, as we rightly divide the Word of Truth. We study such precious information as, written in the Word, with utmost respect and diligence. We give it our daily meditation. It is by inviting the Holy Spirit in our study that we share in understanding and truth. Only in that way we will be able to send forth the Word of God. Filled with truth by Holy Spirit, we supplicate and humble ourselves to Him.

Endeavour, yes wrestle with God like Jacob, for the blessing of the

Truth in Word, deed and actions. Get the true meaning and the true application, not by power nor by might, but by the Holy Spirit. Truth must be divided to all, dispensed in portions in line with the Word of God.

Historical research is important in order to understand culture, classes and subjects. It is fundamental to gather from God's word itself, the exact meaning the writers intended to convey. Take the Bible literally. Receive wisdom and pure instruction.

14   THE POWER OF THE WORD OF GOD

The Word of God has power and is able to make a person wise unto salvation, produce faith; make Jesus Christ known; build people up; give inheritance, is profitable in doctrine; reproof the student; corrects; instructs in righteousness in order to make the man of God perfect for every challenge. Claim that you can take on any challenge! I refer not only to any book of religion, but to the specific book that is the truth about Yahweh the creator of all things. The Bible is our fountain of life and love letter from God! Has it become obvious that the relationship between the child of God and the Trinity, demands intensive input from me and you, brother and sister, in order to have basic knowledge of the letter of God to us?

God's letter of love to us is love declared by our Creator. It is personal to me and you. You must read it. This letter is also our love path to the heart of God, without which God has no opportunity to anoint you as priest, king and to adopt you as child everlasting into His Kingdom. God gave His letter to show the new way of freedom into His presence, which make us the bride of the Almighty, adorn in the perfect love and longing for the intimacy with Him more than anything else. Be alone with God. Love Him. The word of God is quick, and powerful, and sharper than any two edged sword, piercing even to dividing asunder of soul and spirit and of joints and marrow, and is a discerner of the thoughts and intents of the heart. Faith comes by hearing the word. It is the power of God unto salvation. All scripture is given by inspiration of God, profitable for doctrine, instruction and righteousness and is the word of His grace. You can be born again by the word of God which lives and abides and endures forever. The word is the truth of God which works effectually in you, to believe and to live after the Holy Spirit. The word of God thoroughly prepares the man of God unto all good works.

Lord I come unto you to drink in faith from the well of living waters. LET RIVERS OF LIVING WATERS FLOW FROM MY BELLY.

I receive your full anointing of the Holy Spirit and endowment of power from on high. I believe on Jesus, thus I shall do the works that Jesus did. Even greater works than these I shall do; because thou art in heaven, seated at the right hand of the Father, and the Holy Spirit works in me and through me. This I ask in the NAME OF JESUS and as Your Word is the truth, and you said it will glorify Father God, I claim it even as I receive it now. Thank you Lord, Thank you Father, Thank you Holy Spirit. You deserve all honor and glory!

15   BACKSLIDING OR ERRING

*The backslider in heart shall be filled with his own ways.
*Because iniquity shall abound, the love of many shall wax cold.
*Now, the just shall live by faith. *If any man draws back, my soul
shall have no pleasure in him. *If you will not listen to God, *or
obey His commands, *despise His statutes, or abhor His
judgments, *If you break God's covenant, * forget God, *or
forsake Him, *If you provoke Him and turn again to folly, or turn
aside to sin, or turn from His righteousness, *If you trust your own
self-righteousness as you even grow cold in love, *Or if you
become offended and fall away by temptation and allow the cares
of this world to choke you, *If you be ashamed of Christ or tempt
Christ and disobey truth causing you to fall from grace,
*If you turn again to the old bondage of sin whilst you put away
faith and again get to follow Satan, *A man who walked with God
and fought the world, the flesh and the devil but surrendered to the

enemy, *If you recurrently slid back many times and defiled the body as you drew back into perdition, *and stepped away from the hope of glory.

* If you are of those who failed to walk in the Spirit of God and thus served sin, you have problems.

*Backsliding is an awful reality:

There is a surprise for those among us who are of opinion that backsliding is not noticed. It is very important to, and acted upon, by God Almighty.

* God will punish, judge, and condemn His children who persist in sin and rebellion after backsliding. Please do not be a rebel. *Man plays a big role in his own destiny. God cannot tolerate sin. *If man sins and fails to repent, and by that fails to come to God's requirements, that person would be lost. *If that person comes to die without repenting, God is not responsible. *He that believes and is baptized shall be saved; but he that believes not, shall be damned.

* There are many examples in the Bible of people that persisted in a backslidden state. Nadab and Abihu in Ex.19:6. Korah, Dathan, and Abiram Num16: I-3.

Saul the first king of Israel received the Holy Spirit in 1 Sam10:9-13 went into spiritualism in 1Sam 28. He lost the Holy Spirit and died cursed of God.

Brethren, if any person errs from the truth, and one converts him; let him know, that he which converted the sinner from the error of his way, shall save a soul from death, and shall hide a multitude of sins.

Even Judas was once saved and a friend of Jesus Ps41:9 Christ trusted him and he ate of the bread of Christ.

There are many other named examples in the Bible of people who left the faith....

Let not your faith in Christ and the gospel suffer. Study Philippians 1:6 to4:9 and become a subject of God's grace, partaking of His grace, and abound more and more in love.

Approve things that are excellent and be sincere and without offense until the end. Be filled with fruits of righteousness living by the gospel of Christ. Stand fast in one spirit and mind striving together for the gospel. We are not terrified by enemies and are prepared to suffer for the sake of Christ. We have one love and mind with Christ and esteem others better than our self. We let the mind of Christ be in us and obey the gospel as we work out our own salvation. We do all things without murmuring and disputing. We are blameless, harmless and without rebuke among men. O brother and sister, walk by the gospel standard of love, and rejoice in the Lord always.

16   How the famous became infamous

It is as easy to think that the created human being can become arrogant and even after he accepted that Jesus died for his sins, that his thankfulness wanes, and his faith never gets fed in the study of the Word. New patterns of sin develop and lack of knowledge about what it is ''to miss the mark'' never gets exchanged for the pure knowledge and wisdom of the Bible. The snares of the evil one catch up on him. Satan shoots fiery arrows penetrating into the soul where the armor of God no longer is. As applied to Christian warfare they refer to evil thoughts, lusts, passions and temptations of various kinds. Defensive armor as well as offensive armor may be needed. The sword represents the Word of God. Your knowledge of the WORD must be double edged and as sharp as a blade. All are urged to put on the armor of protection of God. Unprotected we get dragged in by sin, making us all again to pay into the account of'' the wages of sin''. As we can remember: The wages of sin is death. That now flashes like a massive neon light over his being. God who cannot tolerate sin is forced to withdraw from the sinner. The Holy Spirit pleads in our hearts, but gets rejected. In due time no sound of His precious soft calling or knocking on your or my heart, is perceived any more. A deadly silence and emptiness prevails in our hearts. No prayer escapes the heart or lips of the backslider any more. Sin is fulfilled and the backslider missed the mark, rather all markers to eternal life, again and again till death. Eternal punishment becomes all that is left when he dies.... Hell prevails and another lost soul strikes the pit. What would be the things that make us guilty? Simply that God's order is: Thou shall love thy neighbor as thyself. Then answer to these examples that the Bible list as the fruit of the Holy Spirit: Love, joy, peace, longsuffering, gentleness, goodness, faith, meekness, temperance and realize that against such, there is no law.

Works that fight with the Spirit of God is thus the works of the flesh and are: adultery, fornication, uncleanness, lasciviousness, idolatry, witchcraft, hatred, variance, emulations, wrath, strife, seditions, heresies, envying, murders, and drunkenness, reveling and such like. They which do such things shall not inherit the kingdom of God.

They that belong to Christ have crucified the flesh with all the affections and lusts. They that live in the Spirit must also walk in the Holy Spirit.

What then? Shall we sin because we are not under the law, but under grace? Surely not as God forbid all sin. Then please do not sin by not loving your neighbor as yourself. Stand in prayer all the way before God to achieve the goal and He would help you.

   It really is possible to err from the truth and thus for a Christian to become a previous Christian and now again called ''unsaved''..... That person incurs the eternal death penalty again. Wake up! Run to God immediately and ask forgiveness! Confess all your sins as God is faithful and just and will forgive you if you repent from your sin.

17   Who were those that erred and fell?

Does it surprise you to hear the first on the list? He surely erred
and fell from a mighty position. He never repented and rather is
still fighting against God Almighty. Satan the very enemy of your
soul!
Lucifer was once sinless. He walked perfectly in the ways God
wanted him to until he sinned even as described in the Bible in
Ezekiel: 28:11-17. Satan is described as the king of Tire, full of
wisdom and perfect in beauty. He has been in the Garden of Eden,

covered with every precious stone. God created him to be the anointed cherub who was on the holy mountain of God. He walked up and down the midst of the stones of fire, perfect in his ways: Until multitude of his merchandise filled Lucifer the Satan, with violence and he sinned. He missed the mark of eternal peace. He has corrupted his wisdom by reason of his brightness. Satan has defiled his sanctuaries by the multitude of his iniquities.

Satan was profane, lustful, and sinful and because of that God casted him out of heaven. Satan lifted up his heart and said that he was a god because he sat in the seat of God. Yet he shall be brought down to the pit, as pride tries to lift the self-up, but can the creature be more lifted up than his very Creator? Satan was created by God Almighty. He is a person with a personal name, personal acts and personal plans to oppose God in the earth as depicted in the book of Job. He has access to heaven and is the accuser of the brethren. He goes from place to place, associates with angels and appears before God. Satan roams the earth, but also carries on conversations with God. He singles out individuals hoping to destroy them and hates good men. He recognizes and envies the blessings of God on people, and seeks to destroy fellowship between God and His children. Satan seeks to cause men to curse God and deny Him, but is limited by GOD in touching His children.

Satan can destroy riches of men which he does to the limit of his ability.

God protects His own children against Satan. Satan has many agents on earth doing his bidding. Satan can send fire from heaven and control the elements and cause storms only when God permits. The propagator of sickness and disease and physical and mental maladies in the bodies of men is untiring in his efforts to destroy good men and cause rebellion, and hold them captive. We know that Satan provoked David to sin. He is the deceiver of all men, and the leader of all sinners and backsliders of the human race. 1 Tim 5:15.

Satan tempts men and provokes them to sin and cause offense. Satan works even miracles and tries to hold messengers of God captive. Satan hinders answers to prayer and set snares for men to fall into sin. Satan can transform himself into an angel of light. He resists others and enters into union with others against God. He sends messengers to defeat saints and hinders the gospel as he steals the Word of God from men lest they should believe it. He blinds men to the gospel and cause diversions, double-mindedness, doubt and unbelief, darkness and oppression, deadness, weakness, delay and compromise, divisions and strife and makes war on the saints. Beloved in Christ Jesus our Savior, did you know what you are up against? That is why we continue in faith, the love of Christ and submit ourselves to the Holy Spirit. Our God is in control.

Jesus is seated as King of kings in the power seat on the right hand of God. Have a Christ like Spirit of love, patience and faith in God. Be sober and keen to have a Godly vision of deep humility of heart and meekness of spirit. Have courage like a lion against sin and sickness, poverty, disease, discouragement, failure and everything else causing defeat in the Christian life. The Holy Spirit gives absolute clearness of the mental faculties and intelligent action in carrying out Bible instructions concerning your duty and personal life as a Christian. Stay away from fault finding, surmising, whispering and slander, and freedom from all the works of the flesh. Know what God's divine will for your life is.
Try the spirits whether they are of God!
The blood of Jesus, our savior, is even sprinkled in heaven to reverse the effects of sin, and the defilement of the Satan. Jesus overcomes sin, hell, and the grave gloriously. Satan is destined to eternal hell, because he caused war in heaven. Michael and his angels made war against this dragon and his angels. But the dragon and his angels did not have the strength, nor was place found for them in heaven any more. The great dragon was cast out! The old serpent called Devil, and Satan, deceiver of the whole habitable world, was cast out onto the earth, and his angels were cast out with
him. Satan is loose on the earth and knows his time is limited. Brother and sister stand fast in faith. Christ our Savior has eternal victory over Satan and his devils. It is in Christ that we overcome and by the Holy Spirit.

18   The 'NOW' Moment

Satan was kicked out of heaven. What is going on in heaven now? 'Now' has come the salvation and power and the kingdom of God, and the AUTHORITY of HIS CHRIST.

This is because the accuser of our brothers is thrown down. The one accusing them day and night before our God is cast out and now is on the earth.

Satan attempts to accuse all humans in order to drag down to hell as many souls with him as would be possible.

Is he successful? For sure he is. Many have turned away from the good news of the Gospel. Thanks be to God, that there are many that follow Christ our Savior ''now.'' Beloved brother and sister the best testimony ever is to be able to say about you'' now I know you fear the Lord! And now I know that the Lord is greater than all gods; for in the thing wherein they dealt proudly, He was above them. Now unto Him that is able to keep you from falling, and to present you faultless before the presence of His glory with exceeding joy, to the only wise God our Savior, be all glory and majesty, dominion and power, both now and forever. AMEN. But now hath He obtained a more excellent ministry, by how much also Jesus is the mediator of a better covenant which was established upon better promises, even some seven hundred and fifty promises. Study the promises of God and stand firm against the attacks of evil. Praise God who put His laws in our minds, and write them in our hearts. God will be our God, and we are His people. We shall all know God from the least to the greatest of us. God will be merciful when we commit injustices against God or man. If we confess our sins, God will forgive our sins and lawlessness, remembering them no more. We sinners overcame Satan because of the blood of the Lamb, and because of the word of our testimony, and we will not love our souls even until death. Write down your testimony! Read it over and go and tell someone of the greatness of God and His Son. We are victorious over Satan by the power of Christ and His blood. Brothers let us rejoice together over our victory in Christ over Satan.

Therefore rejoice as we dwell in heavenly places in prayer and supplication to our redeemer JESUS.

Come now, let us pray:

Lord you said when we were the servants of sin we were free from righteousness, and O how ashamed were we, as we knew the end of those things is death. But now we are free from sin and are become servants to God. We have our fruit unto holiness, and everlasting life because the wages of sin is death, but the free gift of God is eternal life through Jesus Christ our Lord. We accept the gift and rejoice in our Savior and the manifold

blessings of our beloved Abba, Father.
I fear the Lord! My God is an awesome God who reigns from
heaven on earth. He is our Redeemer. The Spirit of the holy God is
in us, for the law of the Spirit of life in Christ has made me free
from the law of sin and death and I walk not after the flesh, but
after the Holy Spirit in me.
I WAS IN DARKNESS BUT NOW I AM LIGHT IN THE LORD
AND HAVE OBTAINED MERCY AND MY MOST PRECIOUS
FAITH BY HIS GRACE.

19   Be Glad Celebrate and Pray Always

I have obtained mercy by the grace of God and the sacrifice of
Christ. This earth is only my passing home.

Because of this I am on my way to heaven. I remind myself that during the feast of tabernacles we proclaim that our life on earth is of passing nature. My body is only my temporary home. Heaven is my home. I am glad that I am travelling through life with the eternal certainty of my salvation. Camp out even as you still are in this passing by earthly tent, your and my body. Jesus showed us that we all will receive and eternal body, even as His body was resurrected.

As I pray, I celebrate His victory over sin, hell and death. We that are saved all Contact God in heaven! He is directly available. Communication with God in heaven via prayer is always open by the grace obtained on the cross and by His blood. The Holy Spirit carries your deepest heartfelt words and feelings personally to God the Father. The prayer of the believer is the fastest moving power in the entire universe. The power of the love of Jesus is carried by His indwelling Spirit from my heart to the heart of God. Thank You Holy Spirit for such amazing Grace- Spirit Speeded, Spectacular Communication System. You operate by the eternal power system of communication: prayer.

Our church needs the latest model of this system to streamline Godly heart to heart communication. As we focus on celebrating Jesus, I pray you would put the power transmission dial on the rapid revive setting.

Please bring into our hearts this revival to set us backsliders in motion.

Let us not forget that Satan was kicked out of heaven! He is angry, but be not scared as he is defeated. The warning is out. All believers who dwell on earth take note and tune in to the power of God the Holy Spirit.

No power can ever match that of God Almighty.

Take the command to be strong in the power of God's al consuming might, prepared and delegated by Jesus to all believers dwelling on the earth, and in the sea. The devil came down to you, having great anger, knowing that he has a little time before he gets cart into the pit of hell prepared for him.. Please compare Dan 12:1, where the arch angel Michael stand up for God's people to Rev 12:7-12 which parallels Daniel's written prophesy. This great wrath of the devil is the severe anger that Satan pours out on the church during the great tribulation. Still we are more than conquerors. We belong to the winning side: Christ who is in you. He is our certain victory.

Beloved, understand the plethora of bad things happening to
Christians at present. There is persecution of believers in Christ.
Paul claims that nothing compares to the great prize that waits for
us. God prepared the prize. Do not lose that grace of God in Jesus
that has your name on it. Claim it back now whilst it is still now.
Repent whilst you are breathing still, as tomorrow has no
appointments for that appointment book called: NOW.
Check James 5:20. Will you be the person that converts the sinner
from the error of his way? Please help that sinner and save him
from death…., Rom 6: 14-23 proclaims that sin shall not have
dominion over you: because you are under grace. Thank God for
that grace so undeserved, Rom 8:12-13 we are not debtors to the
flesh so we do not live after the flesh. Mortify the deeds of the
body through the Holy Spirit our Teacher.   2nd Tim 2:1 Suffer
with Christ, and we shall also reign with Christ Jesus our Messiah.
For my Hebrew brothers and sisters: The Messiah is calling you
now. It is a new day called today.
Dan 12:1Everyone that shall be found written in the Book shall be
delivered.
Rev 12:13-14 Satan, the dragon saw that he was cast out onto the
earth. He then pursued the woman who bore the male child. Two
wings of the great eagle were given to the woman, that she might
fly to the wilderness, to her place where she is nourished there, a
time and times and a half a time, away from the serpents face. This
church would be protected: the church of the Jewish woman who
bore the male child found on the earth during the time of the
tribulation. We love the church working in the Name of Jesus. God
is faithful to His church.
Lucifer, Satan, Devil or the old Serpent is angry and on the earth
wanting that every follower and child of God should fall. Please
Take Heed. Get ready as the second coming of Messiah is
imminent.

20   A third of God's Holy Angels Fell with Satan

The angels of Satan were cast out of heaven with him to become part of the evil on earth and of the evil day.

There is for sure a severe devilish, demonic attack on the church of Christ at present.

Demons are cursed into everlasting fire, prepared for the devil and his fallen angels. It shall come to pass in that day, that the Lord shall punish the host of the high ones that are on high, and the kings of the earth upon the earth. They shall be gathered together as prisoners are gathered in the pit, and shall be shut up in the prison, and after many days they shall be visited. Many of these committed the extra sin of fornication and are now in hell. God spared not the angels that sinned, but cast them down to hell, and delivered them into chains of darkness to be reserved until the Day of Judgment. These angels were fornicating with the inhabitants of Sodom and Gomorrah suffering the vengeance of eternal fire. In Job we read that the sons of God had to present themselves on a certain day before God Almighty. Angels are sons of God and yet those who sin are to be punished forever in hell. So being a son of God does not guarantee you to become a citizen of heaven.

This must make all humans, us, astute to be prepared for the coming of the Lord, because we must be ready and spotless in the eyes of God. Are you washed in the blood of Jesus? Are you filled with the Spirit of God?

Do you do His will? Stand guard and pray. Your Redeemer is coming. Devils fear Jesus, God and the Holy Spirit in us.

Be prepared to do warfare against them. They are prepared to do exactly that against you..... But we are more than conquerors in Christ even as we quote the Bible against their flaming arrows attacking us. Know your Bible. Be able to quote the Word of God as it is the sword of our armor.

Jesus, dear Lord I pray your blood over me even now.   Protect us against all demonic powers that would attempt to attack me, my family and friends. Protect our beloved brothers and sisters in Christ.

Jesus we claim the victory and power on us as your disciples and children by the Holy Spirit as we stand now against Satanic and demonic attacks. Praise and honor belongs to God the Father, and the Son and the Holy Spirit.

21   <u>Demons and unclean spirits</u>

Demons and unclean spirits are real and active in this current world. The word means devil or evil spirit.

Demons were created sinless and in God's grace and favor. Satan is their leader or prince Mt.9:34, 12:24.

Al evil started with Satan, the diabolic one or our adversary, false accuser who slanders. In seventy seven other places the word refers to evil spirits. Humans can be possessed by demons but as Satan has an angelic- body, scholars say he cannot enter bodily into anyone.

However demons are without a body of themselves and do not seem to operate in the material world, except through the bodies of man or beast. Humans can be demon possessed.

They admit that they are doomed to eternal hell and worthy of punishment as did the devils that possessed the two Gergesenes and lived in the tombs. As they saw Jesus, they cried out saying: '' What have we to do with thee, Jesus, thou Son of God? Art thou come hither to torment us before the time?'' Is it not sad that demons recognize and know that He is the Son of God, but many humans deny that Jesus ever lived on the earth? Jesus ordered the devils to go and when they were come out, they went into a nearby heard of swine. The swine ran violently down a steep place into the sea and perished in the waters. Many devils are now in the abyss and will be let out in the last days to torment those people that have not the seal of God on their foreheads. It would be like scorpion stings. May I urge the body of Christ: be ready! Jesus Christ the Messiah will soon return?

Devils believe there is a God and tremble. James 2:19.

God promises to punish every angel or man who sins against Him regardless of being a son of God, or in other relationships.

But, there is a dispensation to come very soon, even in this fullness of time, when Jesus will gather together in one, all things in heaven, and which are on earth, even IN Him.

We who are saved by grace have an inheritance after the counsel of His own will:

* All who first trusted in God should be to the praise of His glory.
* We trusted in Christ after we heard the word of the truth.
* We trusted in Christ after we heard the gospel of our salvation.
* We trusted in Christ after we believed in Christ.
* We were sealed with the Holy Spirit of promise,
* The earnest of our inheritance until the redemption

* Of the purchased possession unto the praise of His glory

*The Bible surely does not teach that we should stop the race halve way through. Rather we must race with all that we have like a well-trained athlete to win the race and the prize of eternal life with Jesus.

There are many examples given of beings fallen from grace. That person may even be you. Check it out!

Come back to Jesus. Do not allow doubt in your heart but conquer in faith in Christ our all sufficient Saviour.

22   Help for the Backslidden Child of God.

Please do not think money is the first goal to achieve happiness.
The Love of Money has brought many a person to sin and is
described as the root of all evil. They that will be rich, fall into
temptation and a snare, and into many foolish and hurtful lusts,
which drown men in destruction and perdition. Some that coveted
after money have erred from the faith, and pierced themselves
through with many sorrows.
Do not believe that consuming food and alcohol in excess will
make you happy as wine is a mocker, and whosoever is deceived
thereby is not wise. Here thou my son…. Be not among
winebibbers for the drunkard and glutton shall come to poverty.
Outward adorning is corruptible; seek rather a meek and quiet
spirit which is great in the sight of God. Sexual lusts war against
the soul. An evil heart of unbelief leads to departing from the
living GOD. Christ is all I need by the grace of God. Be not
misleading by the devil. Sin not. Do not rely on your own
experience and understanding. Hang out with wise people as the
fear of the Lord is the principle of wisdom. You do not have to
please man.
   Stop. Repent. Confess your sins daily.   Focus on Jesus. Study
the Word. Be humble. Spread the Gospel. Pray. Praise God and
give Him the honor. Enter into His presence with thanksgiving.
Worship God Triune with your heart, body and soul. Be inspired to
be those who overcome and win the great price of eternal life in
Jesus! Obey from your heart the doctrine of the Gospel of Jesus as
described in the fullness of the Bible. Faiths believing ye became
the servants of righteousness even as you yield your members of
your body to righteousness unto holiness. Made free from sin by
the blood of Jesus, you become servants. Your fruit unto holiness
and the end reward triumphs as everlasting LIFE.   The wages of
sin is death; but the gift of GOD is eternal life through Jesus,
Christ our Lord:
   Behold I stand at the door and knock. If any man hears my
voice, and opens the door, I will come in to him and sup with him
and he with me. Do you hear the voice of Jesus?   He that covers
his sins shall not prosper, but whosoever confesses and forsakes
them, shall have mercy. Only acknowledge your iniquity, that you
have transgressed against the Lord thy God, and has scattered thy

ways to strangers under every green tree and ye have not obeyed my voice says the Lord. If we confess our sins, He is faithful and just to forgive us our sins and cleanse us from all unrighteousness. Watch you therefore: for ye know not when the Master of the house is coming….. Lest coming suddenly He finds you sleeping. Take heed, watch and pray … Jesus is coming soon, verily I say unto you that this generation shall not pass till all these things be done. Come on. Wake up. Get doing! Run to win. Victory in Jesus!

23   The Work of Demons.

So you say: 'Who cares about demons. I thought this devotional would tell me about my soul and Jesus…'
Beloved, no king can strategize without knowledge of the enemy. You are the child of the King of Kings!
Demons are the enemies of our soul.
Every hair on your head is counted. Jesus died for you!
Why then should you not be thoroughly informed?
Demons can possess people and can cause:
* Dumbness and deafness. * Love of the world. * Blindness.
* Bondage. * Grievous vexation. * Discord. * Lunacy and mania.
*Violence. * Uncleanness. * Betrayals. * Supernatural strength.
*Oppression. * Suicide. *Counterfeit worship.
* Sickness and disease. * False prophecy. * Deceptions.
* And every evil they can…
*Enchantments and witchcraft. * Wickedness. * Heresies.
Take a dictionary and study the meaning of these words mentioned above. You need to know the strategies of the enemies of your soul.
Doing the ungodly is morally wrong, actively bad, wicked and unjust. It is the way sinners pass the limits of God's law of love as given by Jesus. God is not mocked! Do not trespass on the Law of Love!
All these horrible devilish factors listed above can be and will be victoriously resisted and cast out in the mighty NAME of JESUS. So do it in Faith! Take the love of Jesus and live it. Do NOT fear demons! They are totally conquered by Christ. Rely on the Holy Spirit in you and you will conquer. Trust the victor, Christ in you, our hope of Glory.   CHRIST IN ME IS MY HOPE OF GLORIOUS VICTORY OVER THE RULER OF THIS WORLD AND HIS DEMONIC POWERS: ALL TO THE GLORY OF THE FATHER, THE SON, AND THE HOLY SPIRIT!! NEVER BE AWAY AND OUT OF COMMUNION OF HOLY SPIRIT.

24   The Nature of Demons.

For us to understand the enemy, these bodiless beings are evil,
intelligent, powerful spirits. But they are wise. Don't be misled,
they are not human. The human being in front of you could
represent more than one being. So also those animal glairs at
you... They are not angels. They can be cast out. Jesus cast them
out and He is the Ruler of the universe. Demons are inferior to
Jesus and have been sentenced already. Demons are individuals,
and have knowledge, faith, feelings, and even fellowship, doctrines
and emotions and other aspects of soul and spirit. They have
miraculous powers. Demons have personality and are Satan's
emissaries. They are numerous.
Please note that demon possession and demon influence are
different.
Demons can teach, steal, fight, and become fierce and wrathful.
Telling fortunes is one of their functions.
They can even be friendly as in the familiar spirits and come and
go out from a human body as they will unless cast out and rejected.
Demons can imitate departed dead people.
Beloved follower of Christ, remember that devils, familiar spirits,
unclean spirits, evil spirits and seducing spirits are our enemies.
I thank God they are subject to Christ and made subject to
believers by the atonement, the name of Jesus, and the Holy Spirit.
Thousands of them can be inside and rule one man at the same
time. They must be discerned, tested and rejected by believers.
Demons have more than ordinary intelligence. THEIR RIGHTFUL
PLACE IS IN THE ABYSS.
The fame of Jesus went throughout all Syria. The people brought
unto Him all sick people and that were taken with divers diseases
and torments, and those which were possessed with devils, and
those which were lunatic and those that had palsy. Jesus healed
them all.
It is part of blessing of the child of God, who lives by the Holy
Spirit, in the power of the name of Jesus, to take control over
demons and their actions and order them to leave the body they
occupy and send them to the Abyss.

Jesus has full power over demons. Stand against these demons in the mighty name of Jesus. Be in Christ Jesus. Then you can overcome against devilish attacks.

* Be strong in the Lord and in His power.
* Put on the whole armor of God.
* Stand firm.
* Have your loins girt with truth.
* Have on the breastplate of righteousness.
* Have your feet shod with the preparation of the gospel of peace.
* Taking and using the shield of faith.
* Put on the helmet of salvation.
* Take the sword of the Spirit.
* Pray in the Spirit.
* Watch out and be alert.
* Pray in the Holy Spirit.
* Have a broken spirit and be penitent, mild tempered with a gentle spirit.
* Hunger and thirst for righteousness, even with a compassionate and merciful spirit.
* That is a pure spirit, filled with wisdom and mediation longsuffering and forgiveness.
*With the armor of God you can stand against all enemies, withstand the attacks, and quench every fiery dart of Satan. JooHaa! Victory! Even demons are submitted to Christ's authority in us.

Lord Jesus I submit to your Almighty Power as our protector against all evil. In Christ all demons have to obey the children of God.

I claim the protection of God against al demonic forces.

25.   False Prophets

Why should I discuss false prophets? I just do not know! My wife,
who is now with Jesus, warned me not to judge. So hear my
prayer, Lord: I do not want to judge......
'Let this be a word purely by You, Holy Spirit. Take judgment
away from my heart and soul and drive this discussion, not by
power, nor by might, but by Your Spirit. Welcome, divine Spirit of
Truth!   You are invited to share holy divine truth.'
Have we not dried away? Lusted? Desired? Abhorred? Hated? We
were filled with scorning other people.
Does not my soul possess appetites of feelings, emotions, desires,
and passions....? Holy Spirit, change the feelings of my soul, into
the knowledge of my spirit. Then will my inner man surrender all
feelings, and my will, knowledge, intellect and all spiritual powers,
will be unto Jesus and for the purposes of God's Kingdom.   My
life would be love as God is love. My love, soul and spirit will be
immortal love, as my immortal soul is no longer lost. My soul no
longer need to war with lust, as God wants both my body and soul
healthy. That is why He heals me. When my soul leaves my body
at death I will see heaven as I go there. I will see there the souls
slain for the Word of God and for the testimony of the Gospel.''
So beloved, take intense notice of these verses:
Matt 24:11 false prophets shall rise, and shall deceive many.
Matt 19:18 you shall not bear false witness.
Beware of false prophets who come to you like sheep clothing, but
inwardly, they are raving wolves.
This warning is serious and can pertain to anybody. The Bible
includes amongst those also some pastors that destroy and scatter
the sheep of God.
God has told us in the book of Jeremiah to obey God's voice as He
expected of us in the Garden of Eden. I will be your God, and ye
shall be my people. Walk in all the ways that I have commanded
you. It will be well with you.
They listened not, nor inclined their ear to God's voice. They
walked in the counsels and in the imaginations of their evil heart.
Jesus, however, communicated every step along his earthly way

with the Father. He did not rely upon himself, but asked of God. It is of note that shepherds feed their sheep, so pastors must feed the people of God the truth about God. If you have not lead My people unto the place of which I have spoken unto you, to deliver the people of God from the land of the Egyptians and to bring them unto a land flowing with milk and honey, you must repent, and be humble yourself. God has surely seen the affliction of His people, and know their sorrows. Jesus already came to give Himself on the cross, but you fail to preach God's word in truth. By His blood is salvation. By His stripes is healing. By grace and not by anything any person deserved. You fail to live by love or to share the love I offered you. I called you by name. I have spoken to your innermost. I was a conscience to you even as it was still evil. But I awakened it, remember? I purged your conscience, purified your defiled conscience and ask it to be witnessing the truth….. I WILL VISIT UPON YOU THE EVIL OF YOUR DOINGS. Preach the truth as you find it in the Word of God. Invite My Spirit to share the truth and preach the fullness of the truth. I will gather the remnant of my flock out of all the countries and they shall be fruitful and increase. Pastor, you can feed the sheep of God the pure truth, if you desire the truth in your inward side, and if you would desire wisdom from God.

God desires that you would be purged with hyssop, so that you would be clean. He wants to create in you a clean heart and a steadfast right spirit. Have you scattered the flock instead of inviting them into the house of God? Have you chastened them away and have not visited them? Jer 23:2 my sheep were left alone for the wolf and the bear to devour. Is that what your witness is? Did you go out to rescue them from self- destruction? What is left of them that I asked you to pasture? Was your witness the truth? Where you obedient? Did you confess your sins before them? I offer you my blood, the cross, and forgiveness as you confess your sins and repent and sin no more. Then I will revive you and your family and the brothers and sisters with my Holy Spirit. And great shall be the revival. Lo I come soon……

26.   I Will Gather The Remnant...

God said I will gather the remnant of my flock out of all
countries... and they shall be fruitful and increase. Yes, they will
say of the Lord: 'He is my refuge; in Him will I trust.'' If ye
continue in my word, then are ye my disciples indeed. Lord I pray
for that help to continue in Your Word so that I am yours indeed.
Make me to know the truth that sets me free. John 8:32. This very
word was made flesh, the flesh of Jesus! That dwelled among us.
Behold the glory of the only begotten Son of God, full of grace and
truth.
Behold the Lamb of God which takes away the sin of the world.
Please ask for sure the way to go and find that Jesus will answer: I
am the way! If you would ask for life Jesus will answer still: ''I am
the Life.'' Are you looking for the truth to feed your flock? Jesus
says: I am the Truth. Please preach Jesus who is the way, the truth
and the life else none of your flock will reach the kraal tonight.
Yes, no man comes unto God the Almighty Father but by Jesus,
the Christ and the Lamb of God.
O pastor, Jesus prayed to the Father to send you His NAME! It
represents authority. All bow down unto His Name. Confess His
Name to people. Ask anything in His NAME and Jesus will do it.
So ask for the Comforter. He is the gift of God that will abide with
you forever. He is the Spirit of Truth and will teach in all truth.
Jesus prayed for your sanctification through the word of God,
because it is the truth. His Word Is Truth! Stop then to doubt the
Word of God. It is the John 17:17 truth.
Pastor, if you care for your sheep, take this one: Jesus cares. He is
the good shepherd who knows His sheep. He also knows your
deepest needs. He knows the door to His sheep, as He is the only
door into Heaven available to His sheep and you. Think of it like
this: if you do not enter through Jesus the DOOR, sorry, then you
cannot get in. Stop trying climbing up any other way. That is
deception. You get to heaven only through the pierced heart that
shed its blood on the cross at Calvary. Yes Golgotha. That was

there that Jesus prayed for the very forgiveness of the Father '' for they know not what they do.'' If you try to get to the sheep in any other way, you are marked as a thief and killer of sheep. Do not destroy the congregation of God's children, and do not starve them of food and living water. Give them Jesus who is come that they might have life, and that they may have it more abundantly. O Simon Peter, do you love Jesus? Do you love me? Do you love God's Lamb? Simon Peter witnessed there that Jesus knows all things and he cried like a baby thinking how he failed Jesus. Are you lukewarm? Pastor, repent and love Jesus who first loved you. Then please feed the lambs, feed his sheep. Yes feed the sheep! Living for others is really the Christ life after all.

27   Feed My Flock
Pastor,
Feed the flock till we all come into the unity of the faith, and of the knowledge of the Son of God, unto the perfect man, unto the measure of the stature of the fullness of Christ. Speak the truth in love, as you feed the lambs, and study the Word to shew yourself approved unto God. You remain responsible to God all the time. The responsibility is serious in the eyes of the Lord. Shew here is an old English word that means greater clarity of 'showing' than that would be depicted by the word show. The responsibility to pastor the flock is a burden of intersession and fasting and endless prayer. Much grace and love is given unto you, much is expected of you. Knowing the enemy and resisting him always with power from God Almighty.
Thou will show up as the worker that serves and qualifies as a workman that needs not to be ashamed. Pray in deep supplication to be able to rightly divide the word of truth. Stand on the solid foundation of the rock Jesus, and have the seal of comfort that the ''Lord knows them that are His'' and that He requires that every one that names the Name of Christ to depart from iniquity.
Here is some urgent purging to do:
If you love yourself only, then add on to that, loving your neighbor. Be willing to love and to do charity.
Stand firm against covetousness as it breeds greed and murder, poverty and rebellion. It oppresses and cause violence.
Covetousness denies God and leads to injustice, backsliding and deceptions. Please be not defiled even by coveting temptations and lust as it will shorten your life. Purge yourself from boasting, pride and blasphemy. Your parents must be obeyed. Be thankful towards God and people. Be holy as God is holy. Do not accuse people falsely. Live in the power of faith in God, not only a form of godliness. Paul asked us all to pray for him and for all in authority:
Lord Jesus,
 I pray that we would persist in prayer for God's anointed people. Help us all to feed the flock with love, tender care, and the passion

to share the knowledge and wisdom which is your Word. Give us
your passion for sinners to plug them away from hell. Jesus, teach
us to populate heaven as you lead us into glorious victory in our
witnessing!
Holy Spirit, motivate inspire and help every family in the church to
stand up as a strong fortress for the Gospel. Build our church
families on the Rock, Christ the cornerstone of information and our
example.
Delegate to and educate the fathers and mothers to be the hands of
Jesus in pastoring the flock.

28   Prayer for Deliverance

Abba Father,
* Make me a servant in your tabernacle.
* Cleansed by your blood and soaked in your love… overflowing.
* Make me that vessel, used by your potter's hand as an instrument of honor to my Creator.
* This vessel must offer living water.
* Living water from my belly, flow out by Holy Spirit for Salvation of many.
* I am a chosen vessel of God in Christ declaring the coming of Messiah.
* Fill this vessel miraculously with oil, burning in my soul to give glory unto God.
* A vessel in the process of sanctification.
* Let me seek save and honor souls, by the grace of God.
* Make me committed to witness the Good News.
* I am a warrior, spreading the gospel.
* Fill this vessel with understanding in all things.
* I Proclaim Jesus Christ the son of David is raised from the dead according to the gospel.
* I Proclaim salvation in Christ Jesus with eternal glory.
* This vessel is filled with faith, hope and love and thanksgiving.
* Sanctify me for our sacred use.
* Consecrate me wholly to Thee God and your service.
* Cleanse me from sin and defilement.
* Make me a vessel to do God's will and prepared unto every good work.
* I will study the Word of God in detail.
* Let us then flee youthful lusts, follow righteousness, faith, charity and peace.
*Let me worship God with them who call on the Name of the Lord.
* Receive this word of instruction from God in meekness, repentance, in acknowledgement of God's truth.

* Recover us herewith out of the snare of the devil.
* Preserve us, unto God's heavenly kingdom.
*To Him be glory for ever and ever, who has given all scripture by inspiration of God for doctrine, reproof,   correction, instruction and righteousness.
*Man of God that is to make you thoroughly furnished unto all good works.
* Flee from the love of money.
*Rather follow after godliness, faith, love, patience and meekness.
* Fight the good fight of faith.
* Lay hold of eternal life.
* Keep the commandment of Love from Jesus without spot or blemish, not able to be rebuked.
*Expect the appearing of the Lord Jesus in His Second Advent.
*He is the blessed one, the King of kings, and the Lord of lords.
*He is the immortal One, who dwells in Light.
*Honor Him in praise and worship.

29   Sleepers Awake!

Sleep. I need to sleep! What a horrible day was this. After the toil of the day, every muscle is aching.
It is with a sigh that my weary bones recline and invite sleep and rest. With a muscle spasm, resulting in relaxation I dose off...
Restore me as I lay my head down. Restore my body, mind, and soul. O that I can sleep soundly. Adam experienced deep sleep when God created Eve from his rib. God had the appointment with Adam to take a rib, closed it with flesh and made a help for Adam. Adam arose refreshed and could rejoice in the creative miracle, his Eve. Do you rejoice and praise God for your spouse?
Saul, God's anointed king of Israel, slept unguarded. He woke up refreshed after his sleep. He could have been killed. The Lord gives His beloved sound sleep, but He also directs the sluggard to consider the ways of the ants. You see the sleep of a lazy man brings poverty. God asks the sluggard: When will you arise from out of your sleep? Yet he craves a little sleep, a little slumber, a little folding of the hands to sleep.
Rather be taken up by Jesus like Peter, James and John onto the mountain. You will find if you take the trouble to go up the mountain in the presence of Jesus where He is glorified and worshipped, you will see Jesus in heavenly, glistening raiment of glory. You will like Moses and Elias worship Him. You will find Peter, James and John wake up from their heaviness and all they could see is Jesus.
What a way to wake up! Lord I pray that my focus would be to see the glory of Your Majesty. Daniel was in a deep sleep when the angel Gabriel came to inform him about the last days. Touch me as well with the information of these here last days. When Daniel heard the voice and saw the man Jesus's hand touch him which set him on his knees and the palms of his hands. Daniel was put in the praying position. Let this push us into the position of perpetual prayer.   Lord, help me too to be praying and worshipping you as a man who loves you. Daniel was a man greatly beloved by God,

and here he is ordered to stand upright. Lord stand me up too, to be upright, a child of God who experience the beauty of your presence. O let us humble ourselves in the presence of God. Speak to God and listen. I sense His urgent concern. Wake up.
There is no time any more. Now is our salvation. The night is far spent, the day is at hand: the day of the coming of the Lord. Cast off the works of darkness. Put on Jesus who does not slumber nor sleep and is your keeper. HE THAT KEEPS ISRAEL, NEITHER SLUMBERS NOR SLEEPS.
Where for He says: Awake thou that sleeps and arise... and Christ shall give thee light.
To them that believe that Jesus died and rose again, even to them also which sleep in Jesus, will God bring with him. Let us not sleep as others do, but let us watch and be sober.... Rejoice evermore unto the coming of our Lord Jesus, who really cares for you... Look out. Look up. Jesus is coming very soon. Are you ready?
EVEN SO COME LORD JESUS!

30   <u>Be Anointed!</u>

AND IT SHALL COME TO PASS IN THAT DAY THAT THE
YOKE SHALL BE DESTROYED BECAUSE OF THE
ANOINTING. ISA 10; 27

Pour the oil upon us. Anoint us in the Holy Spirit. Give us the
vision to destroy the yoke off those bound by evil. Let us ask the
Holy Spirit to set us free from our bondages and utterly destroy our
burdens. Jesus died so that we can be free. We now stand in Christ,
anointed to be conquerors over the issues of this world.

Messiah is the anointed, consecrated person. Consecrate means to
make sacred. I am dedicated to the purposes of God. For that I
devote my time to God's purposes. I am separated to study God's
people. I am wholly dedicated to study God's Word. I live in the
anointing of the commission Messiah give His disciples to be
witnesses of the Gospel of Christ.

Take that as the working definition of your life and it will change
your way of living into something very special.

Our focus becomes singularly to be like Jesus. He is the Son of
God who does not do a single thing at all that is not cleared first by
the Father. In order to live like that, Jesus goes over every step of
every day with the Father in prayer. The Messiah had His ear
permanently opened to GOD and His word. He lived and worked
on earth as the perfect obedient servant of God and the people.
Now that is devoted obedience! Come let us be obedient to the
voice of God.

Under the utmost of pressure, Messiah did not stop to do the will
of God. Even the death of the cross went exactly as Jesus planned
with the Father and written it down in the Bible. That is also true
that God has a plan of action for you and me worked out. We must
clear every step of the way in His presence. Then only do we know
that we walk by faith the path that God wants us to go. Then God's
purpose for my life becomes mine.

As we walk the path together I grow in love, in friendship and fellowship with Holy Spirit, my best friend.

May the God of Peace;

*That brought again from the dead our Lord Jesus, that great shepherd of the sheep,

*through the blood of the everlasting covenant:

*Make you perfect in every good work.

*To do His will.

* Working in you that which is well pleasing in His sight.

* Through Jesus Christ.

* To whom all the Glory belongs for ever and ever.

* It is God who equips you. He strengthens you, provides for you and completes the task.

* You must only be loyal, a servant and do your job that He calls you for, with your whole heart.

* You can be totally confident in God's equipment. It is custom made for your assignment.

* God anoints you for the job so that you can give all the glory and honor to Him.

* Ask this question always:

* What I am about to do, is that to the glory of God? That will help you to live a life to His glory.

What if you sense that you should not do that you intended? *Stop.

*Seek the opinion of God by prayer and supplication. You might have to go to your prayer friend, or pastor.

*Still do not move to do what God warned you not to do until you hear His answer. He wants to lead you to be His glorious and willing witness.

*Wait upon the Lord. He will supply the answer and then do follow that answer with due diligence.

31   Plug into The power of God

It is the plugging into the Holy Spirit of God that brings the mortal man into the astounding results of miraculous living. This is and must be always to the glory of God and His Kingdom. The results come by the blessing of God and the knowledge it is only by Him. The result is excellent and of an order that the world does not understand. Power requires the equipment and knowledge of the word of God.

Power flows if all is for the glory and honor of God. Success is to be plugged into God's Spirit, moment by moment.

If you know the Love of Christ, which surpasses all understanding and knowledge, you will be filled with the fullness of God. Christ can do exceedingly abundantly above all things that we ask or think according to the power that works in us, all for the glory of God.

What would hinder the power of God to flow through us? Some of us miss out on the plugging in of the Holy Spirit. Deny yourself as it is not you who do the miracle. It is God! Thus humble yourself in prayer, and fasting. Do not blaspheme the Name of God. Honor God who is almighty and all-powerful. Do not trust in your own abilities, as that will separate you from God. Get the power from the Spirit of God. We can do nothing without Him.

Return to the Spirit of God to lead and fill you with the Holy Spirit. The eyes of the Lord are looking for such a person and he will show himself strong for such a person.

Move in the power of the Spirit of God. Work at the level of power that the world is not familiar with, and do it all for the glory of God.

Counter the sign of the antichrist 666, with God's Given Glory, GGG and accept the anointing of the Holy Spirit. Speak out that you accept the anointing of the Holy Spirit, our comforter. Declare that you are anointed. Receive the anointing and function as one of the Spirit filled Sons and Daughters of God. I proclaim my anointing and take my seat up with Jesus at the right hand of God: the anointing is released in me with power.

I proclaim that I am anointed to do my calling at a level that the world is not familiar with. I speak it, and write it to apply it al. I take my seat with Christ at the right hand of God. I speak it every day as it is the anointing that makes the difference in the favor that God gives me, in my work and every aspiration I have. I believe that I am anointed to do those things which we learn from the Word of God, all to the glory of God.

Phil 4: 9. Those things which ye have both learned and received, and heard and seen in me, DO: and the God of Peace shall be with you. Do what Jesus did. Just do it.

While doing our job for Jesus' glory, it will be known and people will honor God. Whilst proclaiming that I am anointed to do my job at a level that the world is not familiar with and proclaiming it is all by the grace of God, to His honor. God's power, and blessing, and provision are breathtaking.

I am anointed to pray, to paint, to preach the Gospel. There is no stopping of the Holy Spirit. I can release His anointing daily knowing that the Spirit of the Lord is upon me to do great things for God and His glory.

I am not great, but just a servant of God and loyal to Him in all humility.

The Comforter which is the Holy Spirit in the Name of Jesus, He shall teach us in all things that Jesus said and is and bring all things to our remembrance.

Because I am anointed with the Holy Spirit, He blesses me doing all things as we speak together. I have the unction from the Holy One. He is the truth and teaches us all.

32   I Surrender Lord

Give in and submit to the authority of the Lord. Give up your
person, rights and possessions to the Lord. Abandon yourself
entirely to the influence of Jesus. You sang before:
  I SURRENDER ALL, I SURRENDER ALL, ALL TO JESUS I
SURRENDER, I SURRENDER ALL!
If you sang that song before in your congregation, then come let us
walk through what this means.
Submit to the authority of Jesus as the first thing you do as He is
the Son of God and God himself. In Luke 14:26 He demands to be
of greater importance to you than: your father and mother, your
wife or husband, your children, brothers and sisters or any other
person even your own life. If you are a disciple of Christ he is the
commander and you the servant. He demands obedience. If you are
a disciple, then Jesus is the head. He died for you at the cross.
Lord, how do I die to self? How do I become so empty of myself
that I am nothing and you everything?   Compare Phil1:19, and
realize that the Spirit of Jesus Christ is using what has happened to
me or you to turn out for our deliverance of our sins so that Christ
can be exalted in my body whether by life or by death. Lord help
me to empty myself of loving myself above all else. Help me
above all else to offer myself up as if I am dead, then my motto
will be what is in Phil: 1:21 Life for me is Christ and to die is gain.
I surrender my life to Christ. I conduct my life worthy of the
Gospel of Christ. Yes! Jesus is the head! And I am dead of self,
empty so that Jesus can manifest in me as the Head. Like Col 3:3
explains, I died and my life is now hidden with Christ in God. I am
IN Christ, as Christ is in
God the Father and the Holy Spirit is in complete control of my
life even as I hear and obey God's voice and Word moment by

moment.
Lord I do not just write these words, I surrender to you.
The outcome of my complete surrender has enormous
repercussions. Jesus takes my place. Instead of seeing sinful me,
God sees Jesus. Wow what a sight! So different and perfect!
Yield up to the supreme God and offer Him your best.
It is absolute and irrevocable surrender of my will.
I surrender my thought process. Take my decisions.
I offer my obedience.
I am for Him and Him alone.
I am determined to be holy because God is holy.
Nothing would stop me from doing exactly what God wants.
I will respond to the tender promptings of God.
I surrender my will to Jesus.
I acknowledge that God knows what He is doing.
I trust in God entirely.
I built my confidence in God.
I trust in the miracle working God.
I am separated to the gospel of God.
I am redeemed.
I am created for the good pleasure of God.
I surrender my heart to God.
Lord I pray make me patient in all abandonment and suffering.
You deserve honor and praise when I am blessed and loved.
You also deserve honor and praise when I am crucified!
I give myself over completely to the disposal of God.
I take no thought for tomorrow, for God knows my needs.
I commit my works unto the Lord.
My thoughts are established.
I commit my ways to the Lord, trust in Him, and He will bring it to
pass.

33   Seed Time and Harvest

There was a favorable beginning after the flood of Noah. The
survivors of the flood went out of the ark, and Noah did the first
building project: Noah built an altar and offered burnt offerings
unto the Lord. And the Lord smelled a sweet savor; and the Lord
said in his heart, I will not again curse the ground for man's
sake.....neither will I again smite any more everything living.
Gen.8:22 Long as the earth remains, seedtime and harvest, and
cold and heat, and summer and winter, and day and night, and
generations of natural people, shall not cease, for perpetual
generations of natural people.
I thank You Almighty God. Despite what is said daily in the news
and in doom speaking, I have an eternal promise to stand on. Take
the seed of all that is edible, plant it, give time, harvest and eat.
Friend, My question arise, have you a garden? Make a list of what
you eat regularly, get the seeds, plant and let it grow over time,
harvest and eat. Plant as much as you can handle. Be generous.
Share with friends, old people, give to orphans. Note however, that
the offering unto God, when Noah build the altar was a sweet
savor unto Him. Then remember the times are near and we have to
be prepared even to be able to eat. The child of God is warned that
we cannot take the mark of the beast on our hands or foreheads.
This will be required of any person in order to be able to buy or
sell food or anything else. Simply be warned and prepared by
stockpiling seed and in ingenious ways make places in flats, back
yards and gardens to harvest food.
    Do not take the chip, the mark of the beast, the 666 or equivalent.

It is the time to stand in prayer, supplication and worship. It is a time to eagerly be prepared to resist the jeopardy of the last perilous days.

Buy food and needed household materials to survive. Do not be afraid! Rather be prepared...

Beloved, many before us have sown seed in the garden of human hearts. Many millions have responded to the seed of the gospel. It has grown in the hearts of many millions who profess that Jesus is there Savior. It is now in the late part of the latter days. It is now the time to go out and bring the harvest in. Let every person who is called by the Name of Jesus gather in the fruit of the labor of the church. Win the souls and bring them into God's house whilst it is summer still. Sickle, for the harvest is ripe and plenteous, but we need laborers.

Pray the Lord of the harvest to send in more laborers. God please send more laborers before the end of the world. In Revelation 14:15it is said that the earth is ripe for harvest

Change the attack of Satan on the end time church to the shout of victory for Christ... Get hell empty, but heaven and the Kingdom of God filled with the souls that you harvested as laborer. We are not saved only to fill a seat on a few church meetings. We are saved to spread the Gospel of God's Grace. Exchange the Satanic 666 with the Glorious Gospel of God's Grace. Jesus Christ our Messiah is victoriously and eternally LORD. In His Name is the victory of the Church.

Love is the language of God. Prayer is our connection to His grace. Intersession for all workers in the field is the command. Support the Churches and Mission workers. Feed the Hungry Children. Stand for Justice.

The coming of the Lord is at hand.

34   Worship the Father, Son and Holy Spirit.

There is perfect unity in the Godhead. Father, it is in humility that I pray. Allow us to understand more about your Trinity. Your unity is perfect and eternal. Your love toward us is perfect. Your grace improves our understanding. Study glimpses from God's word, improve our understanding, love and adoration. We worship. All to Your Honor and glory! God's ways are incomprehensible to the human mind. Lord, there is nothing on earth that could even come near your power. Your power is eternal.

There are three separate persons in the Godhead: God the Father, God the Son, and God the Holy Spirit. Each one has His own personal, spirit body, soul, and spirit. It is to note that the human being is created with a body, soul and spirit as well. Is it not with our souls that we feel and with the spirit that we know? Man was created in the image and likeness of God.   God has been seen bodily by many human eyes. Abraham was visited by the Lord in Gen 18:1- 33 when He visited him in the plains of Mamre. Scripture refers to God more than 20,000 times. There is one God the Father, one Lord Jesus Christ, and one Holy Ghost. Three divine individuals, in divine plurality, each called 'God' and functioning in perfect unity. We can use the word 'God' singularly, or for the united tripled of the Godhead. The Bible speaks mostly in direct speech about God, although some figurative speech also is found. The Father, the Word, and the Holy Spirit is spoken of as one individually or as one singularly because of their perfect unity. Each member of the Deity has position, office, and work. The Father is the head of Christ. The

Son is the only begotten of the Father. The Holy Spirit proceeds
from both the Father and the Son. These three are separate
witnesses of Jesus Christ being the Son of God. God the Father is
the Head and Director of all things done by and through Jesus
Christ and the Holy Spirit.
The Father was in heaven all the time Jesus was on the earth.
Christ now sits at the right hand of God the Father.
Men are taught to go directly to the Father in prayer.

35   More please tell us more about Holy Spirit!

Rather let us pray to receive understanding of what the Holy Spirit
can be to us. Holy Spirit can be in or upon a person. The Spirit can
be taken away from man or depart from man. There were several
outpourings of the described in the Bible, as well as through the
ages. In Zechariah 12:10 the Lord promised that in the last days the
Holy Spirit will be poured out upon the house of David and upon
the inhabitants of Jerusalem. The Spirit of grace and supplication,
and they shall look upon the Lord Jesus, whom they have pierced,
and they shall mourn for Him as one mourns for his only son, and
shall be in bitterness as for the death of his firstborn..
The Holy Spirit will come upon you as you repent of your sin. The
Holy Spirit is the Spirit of grace and unmerited favor. The Spirit
supplicates and pleads with us and for us and in us. He is the Spirit
of recognition. He will cause the mourning about the Messiah.
Holy Spirit will cause bitterness and remorse for the Messiah in the
hearts of Jewish people in the last days. There will be a Spirit of
privacy and personal concern as well as a spirit of forgiveness and
cleansing from sin. In the beginning the Spirit of God moved upon
the waters and the earth. The Spirit speaks by men in 2 Sam 23:2;
Mt.22: 43 and 1Tim 4:1 you can vex the Spirit, Is 63:10
The Spirit can carry men as in 1 kings18:12 and reveals things to
men as in 1 Chronicles 28:12 and Acts 11:28.
The Spirit can come into the mid of people 2Cr 20:14 and instruct
them Neh 9:20 even testify in Nehemiah 9:30 Holy Spirit can enter

into men and make them full of power. Ezra: 2:2
John 15:6 The Spirit has garnished heavens Job26:13 and has
made men Job33:4
The Spirit is a free Spirit Ps 51:12 The Holy Spirit can be
provoked
Ps.106:33, is omnipresent, can judge and purge Is: 4:4, can rest or
remain upon men as in Is 11:12 , Mt3:16 and John. 1:32.
The Spirit is the Spirit of Wisdom, Understanding, Counsel and
Might. Is. 11:2. Holy Spirit is equal with God in sending Christ to
the earth as our Saviour, and He lifts up a standard against Satan.
The Holy Spirit anointed the Messiah. Is 61:1?

36   MY PRAYER

Heavenly Father Tonight I come to repent of my sins. I ask for
your grace, and your unmerited favor. Listen to my supplication as
I plead for your indwelling in my very being. So also I plead for
my daughters and family, the household people and all our helpers.
Jesus is my Saviour. I praise and honor the King of Kings. My
Messiah, O! How have you suffered my LORD! Thank you for all
that you have done. You carried me when I was weak, down and
out. You revealed to me that there is hope. Even when I was
amidst people that did not love me, God instructed me to keep
hope, faith and testify of his love.
Before I was born you loved me and made me. I rejoice in your
love and almighty power. You are my Saviour that purges me by
your blood from all my sins. Your Holy Spirit came to rest upon
me and gave me a new life. O how wise do you make the decisions
of him that believes and does your will. You are the Spirit of
Wisdom, understanding, council and might. Thank You that you
sent the Messiah and that you anoint us to work in Your Kingdom.
Dear Holy Spirit let me never vex you, but rather enter into me and
fill me with your power, by your grace. Be present in me and lead
my daily living from now on till my days on earth are complete.
Purify me, and cleanse me from all demonic action. Holy Spirit is
my teacher, and the Spirit of praise and worship in me. Let my
tongue sing praises and exalt Jesus and the Father and You Holy
Spirit. Let your blessings flow out of my innermost being, like

rivers of living waters, saving souls and filling them with fire and the Spirit of Truth. Let Your Truth set us free and all them that I witness to. Save souls for the Kingdom of God.

ABIDE IN ME. I RECEIVE YOU IN CHRIST JESUS. Holy Spirit, teach me and all of us all things we need to know concerning the Gospel. Bring all things to our remembrance that we have to know to praise and worship the Father, Son, and Holy Spirit. Impart us with your power so that the words of our witness will be followed by signs and wonders. Pour out the latter day rains and help us to get in the harvest all to the glory of God Almighty…

37   SPIRIT OF HOLINESS

O THAT WE WOULD BE LIVING IN THE HOLY SPIRIT. God said that He is holy and we must be too. Holy Spirit: Take me and lead me on. Give me the path of holiness. Wash me in the blood till there is no sin more in me. 0 Just breathe holiness into my being; and I shall be holy….. Breathe in the presence of the HOLY ONE. God's offer to His children is to receive rest in God's peace and in silent adoration accept His love. God's O that love … Every atom of me vibrates by your symphony of love and charity and agape. The love avalanche of my redeemer overcomes me and I find myself leaking tears of adoration and supplication. The desires in me changed and I find myself dead to sin… I Sin no more. My plea changed from separate me, to become; O Father let us be alone. I worship you, and I live in Christ! How I submit to the waters of purification. O it gushes around me, titillating throughout my total being. I die so completely to the sin and destruction of this world that Christ and the Holy Spirit can live and be in me. This is the dispensation of the grace of God. Then, Lord, as I become the righteousness of Christ, please let the desires and the deeds of my body die so that I may live in Christ forever. Holy Lord Jesus, quicken my mortal body because you live as Christ in me. I am a son of GOD, even as Jesus is the first begotten Son of GOD. I can shout loud so that the mountains echo my joy.

The love of God overwhelms me ... Shout to the Lord the
thanksgiving of my redemption! Shout to the Lord my adoration so
that the world can know! ...   Sing out to the Lord praises of new
songs! Let the earth resound! Surely the earth shall rejoice and
praise the glory of the Lord, and from the mountain tops we will
sing the songs of His glory. In songs of glory that brings God's
presence we will be in awe of His glory. His presence and majesty
inspires all the angels to worship His Holiness. Be still as the Lord
is here...... Worship Him. Give Him the offering of your love. So
that we might love our neighbor, our self and O how I love Jesus...
O how Jesus loves me! Abba Father, I adore Thee... Holy, Holy,
Holy are You Lord God Almighty! We adore Thee in the beauty of
Holiness.

38   Holy Spirit: My Best Friend

It is an Honor to tell you more about my best friend and helper
who is the Spirit of grace and supplication. He can descend down
even to my simplistic level...... Mt 3 16 and is prepared to lead me
and you. Be Thou the leader dear Spirit.   Ask the Holy Spirit to
help and even devils will be cast out of people Mt 12:28. Devil be
cast out and leave this house.   Surely the Holy Spirit can be given
to men by the Father as in Luke11:13 this man accepts you ....
And when we get born again John 3:5-8 says that the Holy Spirit is
the agent. He quickens my spirit and can flow out of our innermost
being like rivers of streaming waters. John 7:37-39 He cannot tell a
lie as He is the Spirit of Truth John 14:17 and John 15: 26 It is all
about the Truth.   He proceeds from the Father and the Son. The
world cannot receive Him, yet He abides amongst men forever.
John 14:16 and will teach us all things John 14: 26 bring all things
to our remembrance, He will reprove the world John 16-7-11, and
He will impart power to men Acts1: 4-8. Ye the Holy Spirit will be
poured out in the last days.....
Holy Spirit can be tempted Acts 5: 9 and speaks to men, Acts 8:
29, directs the works of the gospel Acts 11: 12. The Holy Spirit is
the Spirit of holiness. Please Lord make me holy as Thou art

holy... And make me free from sin and death. Rom. 8: 1-4. I believe Lord, please Holy Spirit dwell in me. Christ is in me so that my body is dead because of sin, but the Spirit is life in me, because of the righteousness of Christ. Lord by your order I submit to mortify the deeds of the body through the Spirit of God, so that I may live. Hear my resounding song out of the depths of by being '' because He lives I can live ....." I am raised from amongst the dead, Rom
8:11 and the Spirit that raised my Lord Christ from the dead, also quickens my mortal body from the dead as He dwells in me. Wonderful, glorious, gracious God of love and mercy!!! My sins of my flesh are mortified by the Holy Spirit, as said in Romans 8:12-13. I am a SON OF GOD I TELL YOU! Spirit of God's bears witness of me being a son Romans 8:16. He helps my prayers.

Although He has a mind of His own, imagine He works miracles through believers like me... What loving kindness!
Take the step of faith to pray for the sick and marvel in the healing with praise and worship all to the glory of God Almighty

39   LUKEWARM

Recently during some study and meditation into the precious Word
of God: ....
I had and encounter with the Word of God that was profound. The
words of the Final One, the Amen, came to me. These words were
Faithful and true and came from the Ruler of Eternity and the
Creation of God and were simply this:
* I know your deeds....
* You are neither cold nor hot....
* I wish that you were either cold ....
* Or hot...
* But
* Because you are LUKEWARM
* I Am:
              ABOUT TO SPIT YOU OUT OF MY MOUTH!
Then the Ruler of God's creation looked me straight in the eyes
and asks me: '' Are you lukewarm?''
I was stunned in the presence of the Son of God. Before my mind I
saw reviewed times of active action in the harvest fields of the

Lord. I saw Bibles distributed to many people. I saw young active students going out telling about Jesus our Saviour. I was there. I saw how the Lord provided and how many came to accept Christ as there King and Redeemer. Flitting past were all sorts of activities and times and I saw me later, and it surely was as if my interest was at a different level ... less active.

It seems as if I was sleeping a bit more to rest and that the race was not so important any more. The daily devotions were lacking many days especially when I was behind schedule.

I felt that the Lord was looking at me. I felt that I am wretched and pitiful. I knew that I am poor and blind and naked. I now have a witness that is just like hay burning. As I saw the honest eternal Witness face to face, I knew that my truthful description screams out "LUKEWARM! LUKEWARM! SPIT HIM OUT!

My memory plugged out forgotten shadows, people now dead, that I did not tell about the love of God whose Son died for our sins. Golgotha grinned at me. Accused, it felt that I hated instead of loved.

I do not want to be spat out of your mouth Lord! Please do not spit me out! Forgive my apathy! Create in me a heart of love for souls... Teach me to seed the gospel. Let me spread the good news. I have the desire to care for the eternal salvation of your people. Fire me up to make haste to bring people into your presence......

Lord I Pray with repentance of this sin of being lukewarm whilst people die ....

Then the Lord reminded me that if I do a job for Him to do it well, and I realized that I have not gone up to the cracks in the wall to repair it for the house of Israel, so that it will stand firm in the battle on the day of the Lord!

I repent Lord. I turn to You Lord. Strengthen my spirit and make my flesh ready to fight in your service.

Help me to repair the wall so that it can stand firm in the battle on the Day of the Lord. Make me not weak- willed and acting like some coward! Make my love not like the morning mist or the early dew that disappears. Make my heart not deceitful. Let there be prosperity in the land as you fire us up for victory in Christ. Let the mountains rejoice with seed, and the ground give prosperous crops even as our men and cattle prosper. Bless the labor of our hands. Fill me with Holy fire for your honor and glory. Let me build your house now as the time is come for this. Let me repair the ruins of

your house even before I dare to build mine own...
I turn to You Lord. Please preserve my works from blight, mildew, and hail even as I get changed to be your warrior.
Praise, honor, worship and give al glory unto God Almighty for He is worthy to be praised!

40   Seek the Beauty of Holiness

Solitude deepens the soul....? Seek the beauty of solitude with God. Make the impact that changes the world. Would a man of God then not be holy as God is Holy? We are created in God's image...   We are commanded to be holy... We should live in holiness and even have the fruit of holiness to show as the perfect holiness in the fear of the Lord. Does that not come from a heart blameless and in holiness before God? We are called to holiness and urged to continue in holiness and thus be blessed. Holiness must govern our lives. Come be partakers of holiness. Follow holiness because without holiness, no man shall see God.
Are you set apart for God and His purposes?
God is glorious in Holiness and sits on the throne of His Holiness. He lives in the mountains of His Holiness, speaks in His Holiness and Holiness becomes the house of God. By His Holy power all become overcome with obedience. The highway of his Holiness leads to His capital building and His house is called the courts of Holiness. His habitation is one of Holiness. His chosen are called the people of His holiness. His words are of Holiness. His Spirit is

called the Spirit of Holiness.

He is to be worshipped in the beauty of Holiness.

The church of God is now the show house of Holiness. Follow the inspiring Holiness of God. Let us, by prayer and supplication in fasting come to His House and table, remembering and celebrating the Lamb slain for our sins. It is the Blood of the Son, the Holy one, Seated on High in the most Holy place of honor, that we are mindful of...

In His Presence we stand in total accountability for all careless words, disobedience to authority and every sinful thought and desire of our hearts. Looking up to the Saviour for grace, thanking Him for taking our sins by His grace, we repent of our sins and iniquities. Shall we supplicate ourselves and know to revere God..? Worship Him. Fall down prostrate and tremble in His presence.

The Lord, the Lord is in His House... Repent as it has become clear that we fall short of the glory of God and His Holiness.

Lord I have sinned against Thee. Forgive me! Help me to become more like Jesus. Help me to forgive those that sin against me.

  The Spirit of Forgiveness in His Holiness removes our sins by the Blood which is the offering of Holiness given by our Messiah that washes our sins away. Between the east and the west you will find those sins no more. Be Holy because God IS. Yeah God is Holy.

Lord I dedicate my body as a holy temple unto you.

Take my earthly dwelling and help me by your Spirit to witness a walk in life Holy unto You.

41   Prepare to Meet the King

Holy Spirit:
Take over my thoughts. Redeem them to your honor. Take my
prayers and over saturate them with love. Take my being and unite
it to be one with you. Take myself and make me glorify such Truth
in worship and in deed. Take my days and multiply them for your
honor and purpose.
As I walk, let people experience you. Transform my tongue into
worship. Take my sleep at night and create it to be your vision.
Sweet it is to lay me down. Transform my fears to obeying the
command to only fear God, and I will be a mighty warrior in
Christ. What I can do today becomes the total of every minute I
applied in intense focus on your will. Working in the Spirit is
worth eternal value as saving deposits in my soul account. Holy
Spirit let us fill the account in the distinct, separate, cut above the
rest, majestic account using cleansed lips to utter the praises of
God. Seek souls to be saved. Thou art Holy in every aspect of your
nature and character. Transform both laborer in the harvest, and
the harvested soul into that Holiness of the fullness of the being of

God. Lofty! Exalted! God accepted the offer of Jesus on the cross and we are now saved by grace. Messiah took our sins away. There is no iniquity in the blood cleansed child, that is become one with Christ, one with the Father and with Holy Spirit. The whole earth is become full of that glory spelled 'Jesus', the Holy one of Glory. He is the One called the Alpha and Omega. The Earth has seen His Glory. Holy Spirit I purpose to give your trinity Glory. Is not the ways of a man before the eyes of the Lord, watching us moment by moment. God knows. Let me do and walk GOD'S way mindfully. Bind His law upon my heart. Listen to His commands. Listen up! God is speaking to you….

When you go, His words shall lead you. When you sleep, it shall keep you, and when you wake up God speaks with you. He will give you instruction. He loves you even as you love Him. Your walk gets directed purposely, because: as you seek Him so you find Him.

Walk in the purpose of the Almighty and His instructions. Riches and honor and righteousness are in His presence. The revenue paid by God is more precious than choice silver. Those that love Him inherit substance. He fills our treasures as we become one in vision, purpose and love. As Christ is one with the Father, so are we.   So am I one with the Father, Son and Holy Spirit. I am united with God!

Worship then the God that is before the mountains were settled... God created the earth. God was there when the heavens were made. He established the clouds and the fountains of the deep. Blessed are they that keep the ways of God.

BE THEN WISE: find Jesus. That is to find the favor of the Lord. Jesus is life. The fear of the Lord is the beginning of wisdom. Redeem the time at your disposal! The days are short! Focus! Run to win the most precious prize: Jesus.

Prepare to meet thy God! Holy Spirit please helps me to be focused on eternal life…..

42   David A Man After the Heart of God

Psalm 51
Loneliness is part of the responsibility of a leader. A soul is
purified in the presence of God. Crave solitude in the presence of
God, as it is the place of emotional and spiritual restoration with
God. There we can disengage and discover the perfect protection
of God, with His glorious provision and indescribable presence.
Wisdom surpassing that of Solomon is in God. Holiness, love and
righteousness is commanded us by our Creator. Perfect Holiness is
found in the fear of the Lord and is from a heart blameless in
holiness before God. We are called to holiness and urged to
continue in holiness to be blessed. Let holiness govern our lives.
Let us be active partakers of holiness as without, no man shall see
God...
A king can stand on his balcony and have a good view around ...so
did David. A king at times does not fight in the field with his
mighty soldiers any more ..... So did David. A king has powers
that people have to obey .....   So did David. If the king orders you

to his court you obey ….. So did Bathsheba. Wait a bit. What
happened? God loves this man David.
When the prophet of God waved his finger under the nose of
David some say he was a very, very brave man. The king stopped.
Contrary to many other kings he paid attention. He could however
have killed the prophet. David, like us, had no way to escape the
omnipresence of God. The facts were available:* David was guilty
of murder of Bathsheba's husband. * David was guilty of adultery
with Bathsheba.
Both of these sins made him guilty of the death penalty by the laws
of God as in Gen 9; 6 and in Dt. 22:22-30. David gets penitent
confess his sins and pleads with God for pardon. I am a great
sinner as well.
This is followed with faith by which David anticipates with
gratitude, forgiveness and restoration by the Grace of God. We are
saved by grace alone. David pleaded that the Holy Spirit should
not be taken away from him.
We are all sinners. God cannot tolerate sin, but God so loved the
world that he gave His only begotten Son. In the eyes of God,
David asked for mercy, which is in the plan of salvation for the
world. God extended His loving kindness to any man admitting his
sin with a contrite heart and asking for the tenderness of the
mercies of God by acknowledging his transgressions. As David
repented and asked for forgiveness, even as the penalty of eternal
death was facing him, and the blood of the murdered man was
calling loudly for revenge, God introduced grace. Condemnation
and penalty where to follow…
David realized that he was formed and shaped in iniquity and
conceived in sin. God requires truth in our inward parts. The
wisdom of God speaks in the inner man and convicts us of sin. The
blood of Christ washes our sins confessed, even as we repent.
Bring unto God a broken heart in repentance. David asked more.
Create in me a new heart which would allow us to worship God
anew and enter again into the presence of God. O what grace. O
how wonderful. The King is restored but the babe of sin passed
away and sorrow strikes his heart again. Righteous are you Father,
as you forgive our sins and restore even another child unto David
and Bathsheba….Solomon and You made him wise…..
    Lord I ask for wisdom in my personal life. Grand me the insight
of my folly and flaws so that I may live my life with integrity.
Lord I also ask to be a person with a heart and life after God's

heart, love, holiness and purity.

43   Deception

There are many examples of evil men waxing worse and worse
deceiving and being deceived.
Satan deceived Eve in Gen: 3:4, when he said to this woman
against what God said. He made her believe that she will not die
when she eats of the forbidden food.
There also is reference to deception in 1Cor 6:9 the unrighteous
shall not inherit the kingdom of God and we must not be deceived
that fornicators, idolaters, adulterers, nor effeminate, nor abusers
of themselves with mankind, nor thieves, nor covetous, nor
drunkards, nor revilers, nor extortionists, shall inherit the kingdom
of God.
All servants of corruption relying on their selves and not trusting
the provision of our Lord God Almighty are deceived by the god
of this world called Satan and are disobedient to God Almighty.
We ourselves also were sometimes foolish, disobedient, deceived
serving diverse lusts and pleasures, living in malice and envy,

hateful and hating one another. Evil communications corrupt good manners. Be not deceived; God is not mocked: for whatsoever man sows that shall he also reap. He that sows to the flesh shall reap corruption.

Deceive not with our lips and take heed that no man deceives you as there shall rise false Chris's and false prophets , and shall show great signs and wonders; insomuch that, if it were possible, they shall deceive the very elect. There are those who cause divisions and by good words deceive the hearts of the simple.

Satan deceives the world and the nations and he and his demons are cast out into the earth. There are many unruly and vain talkers and deceivers, especially they of the circumcision whose mouths must be stopped, who subvert whole houses teaching things which they ought not.

Many deceivers are entered into the world who confess not that Jesus Christ is come in the flesh. This is a deceiver and an antichrist.

It is the truth that our Father God is intimately involved with us Ps 139:1-18 He is kind and compassionate Ps 103:8-14 accepting and filled with joy and love Rom15:7 warm and affectionate Is 40:11 always keen and eager to be with me Heb. 13:5 patient and slow to anger Ex: 34:6 Loving gentle and protecting me: Is 42:3 trustworthy and wants to give me a full life Lam3:22-23 Jesus is the truth. The Holy Spirit is the Spirit of Truth and the Word of God is the truth. So we must speak the truth in love as believers in Christ Jesus our Saviour. Pray for the truth of the Gospel of Christ the Messiah to be declared all over the World. Billions still need to hear about the Man of Sorrows who gave His life as a ransom on the cross of Golgotha for whosoever would believe in Him. That is the Message of Salvation, first unto the Jew and also to all gentiles. Share it with someone today and walk the path with that person to grow in Christ.

44   Heartfelt Relationship of Prayer

Pray because we love God and that love drives our desire to be in prayer. Worship God for He is worthy and Holy.
Pray also in the Spirit with an urge to know God.
Pray because God is our source of life and we depend on Him.
Seek Him in prayer and edification all the time.
Pray as we resist temptation and claim victory.
Pray to God to act in salvation on invitation.
Pray on the command of God continually, vigilant, with thanks giving, steadfast with our whole heart without ceasing.
Prayer is vital to all the plans of God on and for the earth.
Pray and fast for greater power. Step out in His Power.
Pray as in talking to God openly and respectfully as a child to his Father. He adores this.

Pray loving the loving God.
Pray loving Jesus, our Friend and Brother.
Pray in the Name of Jesus, representing all power and might in
heaven and the earth, the supreme power of all eternity!
Pray in full acknowledgement of the Holy Spirit as our Teacher,
Guide and Comforter.
Pray that the blood of Jesus cleanse us of all our sins so that we
can speak to God.
Prayer enters His gates with thanks giving for forgiven sins.
Prayer thanks God for being in my life.
Prayer thanks God for making me a child of God.
Prayer talks about my needs.
Prayer thanks God for all my answered prayers.
Prayerfully forgive those that have sinned against us.
Prayerfully forgive all who offended us and hurt us.
Prayerfully see yourself dead to sin and sinless in the eyes of God
by the blood of Jesus Lord teaches me to pray persistently.
Continue praying in and out of season, talking to the Almighty
God holding our hand in Abba Fatherly Love never leaving or
forsaking His children.

45   The New Testament Ministry

Now thanks are unto God, which always causes us to triumph in
Christ, and makes manifests the savor of His knowledge by us in
every place. Ye are complete in Him, which is the head of all
principalities and power. Beware lest any man spoil you through
philosophy and vein deceit after the tradition of men, after the
rudiments of this world even the principles and ways contrary to
the gospel. As ye have therefore received Christ Jesus, the Word,
so ye walk in Him. Rooted and built up in Him. Stabilized in faith
as you have been taught, abounding in faith and in thanks giving.
Whosoever is born of God, overcomes the world even by our faith.
He who believes that Jesus is the Son of God overcomes the world.
We know that all things work together for good to them that love

God, to them who are called according to His purpose. I am called
into the ministry of following God's moment by moment present
guidance. God did foreknow, He even did predestined them that
He called, to be conformed to the image of His Son. Jesus is thus
the first borne among many brothers whom He called, justified and
glorified. The death of Christ set us free of condemnation seeing
that Christ died for our sins. He is raised, is seated at the right hand
of God in heaven. Here Christ makes intercession for us, as our
Eternal High Priest after the order of Melchizedek. He is our King
of righteousness. Who shall separate us from the love of Christ?
Would Tribulations, distress, persecution, famine, nakedness or
peril or sword? Think about that. For Thy sake we are killed all the
day long; we are accounted for sheep for the slaughters. Nay! In all
these things we are more than conquerors through Him that loved
us. I am a winner by the grace of God. I am persuaded that: neither
death, nor life, nor angels, nor principalities, nor powers, nor
present things, nor things to come, nor height, nor depth, nor any
other creature shall be able to separate us from the love of God,
which is in Christ Jesus our Lord.
This is a Soul saving ministry as we are unto God a sweet savor of
Christ in them that are saved, but a soul damning ministry to them
that deny such grace offered to them. Mk16:15-16
We are a sincere and truthful ministry not corrupting the Word of
God as we speak in the sight of God in Christ Jesus our Saviour:
Now the Lord is that Spirit: and were the Spirit of the Lord is,
there is liberty.
Be that ministry commended by God and not commended by
ourselves, written not in ink, but with the Spirit of the Living God.
Ye are our epistles written in our hearts. Our sufficiency is of God
and to Him goes all the praise and honor and glory forever.
This ministry is of the New Testament, not of the letter, but of the
Spirit for the letter kills, but the Holy Spirit gives life.
Follow a ministry of glory and righteousness by patient
continuance in well doing in righteousness and obedience to the
truth. Shun evil. Work what is good and do not be contentious. Let
there be glory and honor and peace to every man that works good
for the Jew first, as well to the gentile, for there is no respect of
persons with God. Whatever ye shall bind on earth, shall be bound
in heaven. If two of you shall agree on earth as touching anything,
that they shall ask, it shall be done for them of my Father which is
in heaven. God's ministry of glory is enough for us. There is no

ministration of condemnation, for God's kingdom is not meat or drink, but righteousness and peace and joy in the Holy Spirit.
Proclaim a ministry of Hope, Light and Liberty in great plainness of speech, removing the veil upon our hearts by turning to the Lord Jesus our Messiah and Redeemer. Now the Lord is that Spirit and where the Spirit of the Lord is, there is Liberty.
Proclaim a ministry of constant transformation, were we with open face behold the glory of the Lord! We are changed into the same image from glory to glory even as by the Spirit of the Lord. Keep on submitting to the transformation, edification and beholding the glory of the Lord.
Stand fast in the liberty wherewith Christ have made us free, and be not entangled again with the yoke of bondage.
For the law made nothing perfect, but the bringing in of a better hope did, whereby we draw near to God by our high priest Christ Jesus after the eternal order of the king of Salem.
Love God above all else and proclaim it in audible words to your neighbors, even as you love that very neighbor with the sharing of the blessing of the Word of God.

46   Lord be Thou our Ministry

An honest ministry that is excellent, with an excellent treasure of Ministers functions by preaching the power of God and not of us. We must give all honor be to Father God. These workers in the kingdom become fishers of men. They labor to shine as lights in this world of darkness. Like the Apostles they share the gospel to the people all over the world as prophets, teachers, pastors, evangelists. As ambassadors of the Kingdom of God, they represent Christ. Do not the angels serve the churches?
Lord, make the members of Your Church mighty warriors like David, to defend the faith valiantly. Lift up the elders, to be men of God, messengers of Your Gospel truth to churches and people. Let them walk the walk that is the witness. What then is a Minister of God and of Christ else than a worker, laboring together with

Christ, reconciling the world unto Jesus Himself, that we might be made the righteousness of God in Jesus our redeemer. Child of God, minister then the gospel, the Word, the New Testament, the church in righteousness, remembering your end shall be according to your works. Be then made a minister, according to the gift of the grace of God given to you by the effectual working of the power of God. Preach the unsearchable riches of Christ, by the manifold wisdom of God. Be that student of the wisdom of God. For this cause, bow your knees unto the Father that He would grant you according to the riches of His glory, to be strengthened with might by the Spirit in your inner man. Let Christ dwell in your hearts by faith. Be rooted and grounded in Love as God is Love. Be able to comprehend and share with all saints the breadth, length and depth and height of the love of Christ, and be filled with all the fullness of God.

Study the function of the Church as overseers, preachers, servants of God, Jesus and the Church. Study and seek the fullness, presence and miraculous signs and deeds of Holy Spirit. You are Stewards of God, His grace and the mysteries of God. Do you understand the mysteries of God? Holy Spirit is the Teacher to learn from in due diligence.   Witness and work together with God by sowing seeds of

God's Word, as it never returns to Him void. Shepherd the flock under your care. Do al to the Glory of God.

Minister, it is hard for thee to kick against the pricks. It is Jesus calling that you would rise and stand upon your feet for He appeared unto you for this purpose to make thee a minister, a subordinate to God the Father, God the Son, God the Holy Spirit and to be a witness and prepared to be martyred for your faith in Christ. Witness to those who need Christ those things in which Jesus is declared. Holy Spirit will confirm unto thee, deliver thee and now send thee in God's mighty Name to:

*Open their eyes *turn them from darkness to light * from the power of Satan unto God * that they may receive forgiveness of sins * and inheritance among them which are sanctified by the faith that is also in me.

Did not Reinhart Bonke say it is all about winning souls to fill heaven? Yes, empty hell and fill God's heaven with righteous souls for eternity and on...

Like all children of God, we are all witnesses and excellent ministers of the Gospel as we witness in the Holy Spirit. All rise to

proclaim the witness of faith in Christ Jesus, all to the glory of God
Almighty!
What is your personal witness concerning your redemption? Share
it humbly. Share with those who seek such brotherly support.
Share daily as every day proclaims the glory of God. Recognize
the grace of God on your life and proclaim the sweet presence of
the Lord. The more God is praised by your proclamation, the
greater flow the streams of living water from Gods heart to your
heart and to the heart of the soul of the person you witness to. Be
God's witness to many people. Be God's witness by seeking divine
appointments with people by God's grace. This will happen as you
pray God to arrange appointments with people that He wants to
pursue even by using you. Is that not uplifting to work with God in
His kingdom? Holy Spirit will help you in setting all this up to the
glory of God.

47   Honesty in Ministry.

Therefore seeing we have this ministry of serving and have
received mercy, we faint not, but have renounced the hidden things
of dishonesty, not walking in craftiness, nor handling the word of
God deceitfully, but by manifestation of the truth, commending
ourselves to every man's conscience in the sight of God.
We are providing for honest things, not only in the sight of the
Lord, but also in the sight of men. Look out for men of honest
report, full of the Holy Ghost and wisdom. Them we may appoint
over this business. Recompense to no man evil for evil. Provide

things honest in the sight of all men as God's command to Christians and the world. Supplications and prayers and intercessions and giving of thanks must be made for all men, kings and all that are in authority, that we may lead a quiet and peaceable life in all godliness and honesty. This I pray for the person receiving the gospel seed into an honest and good heart, that having heard the word, you would keep it, and bring forth fruit with patience as you live by it. For those we praise the Lord and keep on praising and worshipping our Abba Father of grace. Have your conversations in honesty. Let people by noticing your good works, glorify God in the day of visitation. Is not our hearts known to God? He is with our every step. Let us walk honestly, as in the day; not in rioting and drunkenness, not in chambering and wantonness, not in strife and envying.

Lord; let every step I make in honesty, eternally glorify your name.
Study the Word of God. Be quiet, and do your own business. Work with your own hands. Walk honestly toward them that are without, that ye may have lack of nothing. God really supplies all our needs. Pray for one another to be honest, trustworthy and serving blamelessly. Pray for us; for we trust we have a good conscience, in all things willing to live honestly.
Keep the financial books perfectly and of a high standard that the world and God could give you a crown of glory for you to offer God. Keep the records and minutes of your actions and deeds as a minister, so that all can read and glorify our Father who art in heaven. Cast your crowns to the thrown of the eternal God.

48   An Unselfish Ministry

I pray that we could share a ministry that is unselfish and not hidden from anybody especially not to those of us who do not know Jesus yet. It is clear in my mind that the ruler of this world is very actively blinding the minds of many people so that the glorious light of the Gospel of Christ cannot shine onto them. Let us preach the good news of salvation. We are servants for Jesus' sake. God commanded the light to shine out of darkness, hath shined into our hearts. He gives the light of the knowledge of the glory of God to shine on us and through us. Witnesses of the Light of the gospel of Jesus Christ transform people of the darkness into the light. The Holy Spirit takes the sinner to repent and to accept the sacrifice of the blood of reconciliation shed by Jesus at the cross. The sinner gets free and God accepts him as a newborn child of faith. A sinner becomes reconciled because God sees no more sins on that previous sinner. We have the power to bind things on earth and it shall be bound in heaven. The excellence of the power of God belongs to Him. In our ministry of suffering as depicted in second Cor 4:8:12 We are troubled on every side, but not distressed, perplexed but not in despair, persecuted but not forsaken, cast down but not destroyed, always bearing about in the body the dying of our Lord Jesus, that the life of Jesus might be made manifest in our body. Thus our witness can not only be heard, but also seen by our example. Jesus please clean my example that I shine through my life to honor God's glory. My steps in life are made all to the glory of Abba Father as Holy Spirit make my steps in life all to the glory of Abba Father. We are always delivered unto death for Jesus sake, that the life of Jesus might be made manifest in our mortal flesh. So then death works in us but life in you who observe the life of Jesus in me.

Take your bold and faithful ministry and share in the Spirit of faith. We also believe and therefore speak up boldly. Holy Ghost, who resurrected the Lord Jesus, shall raise us up also and shall present us with Christ. All things are for your sakes so that the abundant grace through thanks giving redounds to the glory of God.

Hear my Ministry of eternal things: We faint not to the cause of the glory of God. Despite the fact that our outward man perish even as our body gets corrupted and destroyed, we still work for the sake of winning souls to glorify God, even if we have to suffer all things and trials, still our soul and spirit are renewed day by day in knowledge after the image of Him that created a new man with a sound mind and true knowledge according to the original pattern of God who created him. I have an eternal soul. It is better to be with God for eternal life. Nothing now in this corrupted world can match up to the standard of eternal life with Jesus. Our light affliction is considered momentary as compared to eternity. Any afflictions are but slight compared with the eternal weight of glory one receives in exchange for our sufferings in heaven. We look not at the things which are seen and temporal, but at the things which

are not seen and eternal!
O what a confident ministry we have for the future. According to
prophecy we will be living in eternal glory. God's children live in
His presence. We know that when our earthly house, this body, is
dissolved we have an eternal house. God prepares our house. We
desire to be clothed upon with our heavenly attire so that we shall
not be found naked. That is what God has in plan for us who has
given us His Son, the first fruit of the Spirit, Jesus Christ as our
proof. We will be resurrected and will put on immortality. Because
we believe and walk by faith, we are confident and willing to be
present with the Lord eternally. Jesus secures our eternal life. But
you have to accept His sacrifice on the cross for your sins.

49   A Hard Working Ministry

We labor, whether present or absent, that we may be accepted of
Him. For we must all appear before the Judgment seat of Christ.
Every one may receive the things done in his body according to
that he hath done, whether good or bad.

Knowing therefore the terror of the Lord, we persuade men; but we are made manifest unto God. Righteous and unrighteous alike will stand before Christ and receive the recompense of our lives.

We should not glory in outward appearance, but honor Him from the depth of our hearts. Remember we are saved by grace and serve in thanksgiving. We are servants ordered to work in the field of our master. For other foundation can no man lay than that is laid, which is Jesus Christ. Now if any man build upon this foundation gold, silver, precious stones, wood, hay, stubble; Every man's work shall be made manifest: for the day shall declare it, because it shall be revealed by fire; and the fire shall try every man's work of what sort it is. If any man's works be not burnt up which he has built thereupon, he shall receive a reward. If any man's work shall be burnt, he shall suffer loss: but he shall be saved; yet so by fire.

Hard working ministry worker, ye are the temple of God and the Spirit of God dwells in you....

If any man defiles the temple of God, him shall God destroy; for the temple of God is holy, which temple ye are. I praise God for my body, God's temple. I live holy in His palace of holiness.

Knowing about this Judgment Seat of God, the Terror of Christ:

* Judge not thy brother.
* Persuade men to repent as every knee shall bow and every tongue shall confess to God.
* Everyone will give account of himself to God.
* We are all made manifest unto God.
* We are made manifest in your conscience.
* Let us then glory in our hearts to God.
* Let us glory beside ourselves for the sake of them to be saved.
* Be of a sound mind and bring your body into subjection.
*This way the minister would not himself be a castaway....
* Rejoice in the Lord.
* Have no confidence in the flesh.
* Apostles, prophets, evangelists, pastors and teachers, all, work for the perfection of the saints:
* For the working of the ministry.
* For the edifying of the body of Christ.
* Till we all come in the unity of faith.
* Of the knowledge of the Son of God, unto a perfect man.
* Unto the measure of the stature of the fullness of Christ.
* Joy and rejoice in Christ even as you trust Him with your life.

* Care for and seek the things of Jesus.
* Speak the truth in love and grow up into Christ in all things. Not with eye service, as men pleasers,
*Speak the truth as the servants of Christ, doing the will of God from the heart.
* With good will do service as to the Lord and not to men.
* Knowing that whatsoever good thing any man does, the same shall be done unto him.
* Be strong in the Lord and in the power of His might and put on the armor of the Lord...
* Work out your own salvation with fear and trembling as God works in you to will and do His good pleasure.
* Do all things without murmurings and disputing that ye may be blameless and harmless.
* Be the sons of God without rebuke.
* Let your light shine.
* Hold forth the Word of Life.
* Run to win the race.
*Tire not in your labor.
*Fathers and mothers let your house be a temple to raise your children in the fear of the Lord. Like priests and kings educate your children to know the Word of God so that you all will be blameless and glorious unto God.

50   A Ministry of Reconciliation

Let us reconcile, harmonize conflicting matters, become friends again and accept that all power is given unto Jesus, both in heaven and in the earth. That is why he gave us an order to teach all nations the gospel, baptizing them in the name of the Father, and of the Son, and of the Holy Ghost, teaching them to observe all things whatsoever I have commanded you; and lo I am with you always even unto the end of the world.

Go ye and preach the gospel to every creature.

* He that believes and is baptized shall be saved.
*He that believes not shall be damned.

And these signs shall follow them that believe;
* In my Name shall thy cast out devils.
* They shall speak with new tongues.
* They shall take up serpents.
* If they drink any deadly thing, it shall not hurt them;
* They shall lay hands on the sick and they shall recover.
* So then the Lord was received up into heaven and sat on the right hand of God.
* The disciples of Jesus went forth, and preached everywhere.
* Lord working with, and confirming the Word with signs and wonders.
* You shall receive Power after the Holy Ghost is come upon you.
* Ye shall be witnesses unto me both in Jerusalem, and in all Judaea,
* And in Samaria, and unto the uttermost part of the earth.
* Jesus wants to reconcile his creation with his GOD.

The love of Christ urge us to understand the principle that He died on the cross, taking the sins of all onto Him. That paid the death penalty for the sins of mankind. One person took the sins of all in the place of all. That paid the penalty once and for ever.

That is why I and we all now live for Jesus. We were bought with blood of the Son of God. He is the King of kings. It is the most expensive blood available in all times, and is powerful and dramatic in action. I dare any sinner to ask forgiveness for their sins. Repent of that sinful life, turn around and experience that if any does that, he is a new man in Christ. He is reborn into a new creature. Old things have passed away and behold, check it out, all things are become new. God of our creation has reconciled us to Himself by Jesus Christ and has given us the ministry of reconciliation.

We the prodigal children, that went our way to squander and sin, can in coming back to the Father, loving , waiting for me and you be accepted with yearning open arms back into the feast of restoration as a child. If we do remember the last phase which is restoration of the relationship with our brother and did that in humility we have arrived home. We are now ambassadors of Christ with the love and friendship of God offered by the sacrifice of Jesus to reconcile us forever. We come from enmity to be saved by the blood. We previously were in eternal condemnation of sin to eternal hell. Now we have no more sin and are going to eternal heaven. There is then no more hate towards even our brothers and sisters. There is now love. People that we hated as our enemy, become the one to minister the love of Christ to. Fight for his sole! Paul worked in the ministry of reconciliation and showed the way to eternal life with Jesus. That is the message that every sinner needs to hear. That is our victorious crown to work for.

51   Entreating Ministry

This is an earnest request. Like Paul I would want to appeal to you as if standing before a judge knowing all related to the Jewish people and also the gentiles like me. I beseech you by the very mercies of God and by the Name of our Lord Jesus Christ, even as Paul did who was a prisoner of the Lord, beseeching people to walk worthy and to abstain from fleshly lusts which war against the soul to kill or to take captive. We are ambassadors of Christ. God beseech you by this very word to be reconciled to Him. God made Jesus to be sin for us. Jesus knew no sin, but took our sins on Him. That made us righteous before God even in what Jesus did on the cross for our sins. He became our eternal offering for our sins. Please accept that He paid the price for our sins. This offer is free, the price is paid, and the present is worth eternal grace and blessing.... Walk worthy of the vocation wherewith ye are called with all lowliness and meekness. Be not easily provoked. Rather accept suffering, for bearing one another in love, endeavoring to keep the unity of the Spirit in the bond of peace. Like that flesh of the bullock of Exodus 29:14 as well as his dung was burnt with fire, as an offering outside the camp: that sin offering, so was Jesus a sin offering outside the camp on Golgotha.

Jesus came in the totality of the Book about Him, the Bible, to be an earnest request, a pleading ministry for the souls of sinners: THEN JESUS SAID, LO: I COME IN THE VOLUME OF THE BOOK WRITTEN OF ME. I DELIGHT TO DO THY WILL O MY GOD: YEA THY WILL IS WITHIN MY HEART. I HAVE PREACHED RIGHTEOUSNESS IN THE GREAT CONGREGATION: LO, I HAVE NOT KEPT SILENT WHEN I SHOULD HAVE SPOKEN. MY LIPS SPOKE THE TRUTH O LORD, THOU KNOWEST. I HAVE NOT HID THY RIGHTEOUSNESS WITHIN MY HEART; I HAVE DECLARED THY FAITHFULNESS AND THY SALVATION. I HAVE NOT CONCEALED THY LOVING KINDNESS AND THY TRUTH FROM THE GREAT CONGREGATION.

We are workers with Christ. I beseech you to receive the grace of God in Christ for He says: I have heard thee in a time accepted, and in the day of salvation have I secured thee.
NOW IS THE ACCEPTED TIME.
NOW IS THE DAY OF SALVATION.
NOW, NOW, NOW PLEASE, TOMORROW MIGHT JUST NOT COME.

52   A BLAMELESS AND APPROVED MINISTRY

We are responsible in the eyes of God for our ministry.   Are you
the reason that the member is no longer attending?

Lord, do I stand clean or guilty? I pray that you would open my eyes to anything that would tarnish this ministry. I accept my responsibility.

In all things approve us as ministers of God in much patience in afflictions, in necessities, in distresses, in stripes, in imprisonments, in tumults, in labors, in watching, in fasting, by pureness, by knowledge, by longsuffering, by kindness, by the Holy Ghost, by love unfeigned, by the word of truth, by the power of God , by the arm of righteousness, by honor and dishonor, by evil report and good report, as deceivers and yet true, as unknown and yet well known, as dying and behold we live, as chastened and not killed, as sorrowful yet always rejoicing, as poor yet making rich, as having nothing yet possessing all things.

The Hebrew word ra means affliction is never translated as sin but more something bad or evil, adversity, calamity, grief, sorrow, wretchedness. The idea is that God made sorrow, misery, wretchedness as the fruit of sin even by what you sow, so shall you reap. Afflict denotes a physical disease in some six times and follows the law of sowing and reaping. The time of affliction of a person is determined by God. God is not keen to afflict. Some men are born in affliction even as saints could be appointed affliction to suffer. Paul accounts his afflictions small as compared to the glory of going to be with the Lord eternally.... Affliction is often severe but is temporary. Please be not hardened by our afflictions. Rather count it as blessings and draw closer to God's heart. Afflictions can be caused by sin, backsliding, a sharply misused tongue and even resentment, pride, and impenitence. Examine your heart!

Do not mistreat others or harden your heart. Idolatry, forgetting God and hypocrisy all could land the affliction of the Lord who plans it to work good in one. Would that not hide pride from man and demonstrate that God is faithful and testing our sincerity? God is refining, purifying, and pruning us to improve our fruitfulness and increase His power and grace unto us.

O that we shall come back to the Lord our God. He is humbling us and correcting our paths even making an example of us to manifest His abundant love to. All this can increase His eternal reward towards us as we learn obedience and truth. God will hear the afflicted! Save them, and have mercy on them. He will deliver them from fear and out of all their troubles, uphold them, reward them and be their refuge. He knows our weakness and as He hides us and considers us, His Grace Will Be Sufficient for us..........

53 WHAT! JESUS RESURRECTED?

Yes Indeed! God sent His Son to the earth in the fullness of time, to live a life that is perfect without sin or blemish. Then Jesus, the

Son of God, would be offered as atonement for the sins of
mankind. He would be like a lamb lead to be slaughtered. He
would be despised, bodily tortured beyond recognition and
crucified on a cross, the symbol of being accursed. He would be
bleeding all over from multiple wounds, and yes, Jesus died on the
cross. He was laid in His grave. He was restored to life as revived,
yes, as in rising again from the dead after the third day. Did you
not understand?
Why are you troubled? And why do thoughts arise in your hearts?
Jesus is alive! He rose again! He said to His disciples: ''I am the
same Jesus that walked with you for several years, not a ghost or a
spirit, as I have a human body of flesh and bones. The physical
resurrection of Jesus declared God in a heavenly body with hands
and feet. The very same Jesus that walked the earth in person is the
image of God. His disciples handled and saw Him eating fish and
honeycomb after His resurrection. That is glorious! That body that
was dead is now alive but O so glorified… They held His hands
and feet like little curious children, looking at Him in amazement
and awe. They surely saw Him alive and could thus witness the
very fact to all believers. Jesus is resurrected and there was no
body in the grave to decay! Why seek you the living body among
the dead? He is in His glorious body and is alive.
Jesus drew near to His disciples and sat and ate meat with them
and they knew it was Him. Jesus eats with his glorious new body.
Angels saw Him alive. He walked amongst His followers and
made twelve appearances to hundreds of eye witnesses.
Please note that I Cor15 makes it clear that if anybody does not
believe in the physical resurrection of Jesus Christ, that person will
be lost. Physical resurrection proves to be a crucial aspect of the
Gospel of Christ.
Sorry I should have made the point that; there is a spiritual
resurrection. The spirit of a human becomes quickened from
trespassing and sins. That means that spirit of that human being is
changed, or renewed. The Holy Spirit is sent by the Father and
Jesus with the task to convince people of sin, convict them by their
conscience, refute and expose them, to bring to shame the person
so reproved. He will convince the world of sin, and of
righteousness, and of judgment. Transgressing the laws of God as
found in His Word is called, sinning. If we commit a sin, we
become sinners or if I commit a sin, I become a sinner. The Bible
makes it plain that we humans all have sinned, as in breaking a

religious or moral law or offence against a principle or standard. It is a sin not to believe on Jesus, who is our righteousness. If we believe not we have no righteous standing before God. That unrighteous standing leads to the judgment of God making us partakers of the way of the devil.

Please Holy Spirit, work in our hearts that we will have Godly sorrow in our hearts to turn away from our sins and carefully clear ourselves from indignation, fear, vehement desires, and revenge. Refresh our spirit by your indwelling dear Holy One. Jesus said that we must repent of our sins or we shall perish. We must humble ourselves before God and ask Him to be merciful to us as sinners. This is personal between each of us and God. I cannot do that for your sake. I must do that. I cannot do that for your sake. I must do that myself. You cannot do that for my sake. You have to humble yourself before God and plead His mercy and forgiveness for you.

We must not exalt ourselves before God. Confess with your mouth the Lord Jesus, and believe in your heart that God has raised Him up from the dead and you will be saved. For with the heart man believes unto righteousness and with the mouth confession is made unto salvation. It is the goodness of God that leads us to repentance. It is God's faithfulness to His Word and the perfect offering of Jesus on the cross that secure our salvation unto righteous standing before God. If we confess our sins, He is faithful and just to forgive us our sins, and to cleanse us from all unrighteousness. In every nation he that fears Him and works righteousness, is accepted unto God. The salvation is given to all that believe the Gospel of Christ, all over the world. Peace is found in Jesus Christ as He is Lord of all.

Then follows the gift of power after the Holy Ghost is come upon you and ye shall be witnesses unto Jesus both in Jerusalem and in all Judea and in Samaria and unto the uttermost part of the earth. Jesus sends the promise of Abba Father unto us. Come Holy Spirit as Promised. Behold now is the time accepted and now is the day of salvation.

54   Obedience

The demand God Almighty asked of Adam and Eve in paradise is
to be obedient. Gen 2:16. In Gen 3:11 God checks on Adam and
Eve concerning this command which stands out as the great
required virtue of paradise. To be in paradise requires that man
must be obedient to God. Adam and Eve failed the obedience test
and could not eat of the tree of life. God did not want His paradise
to be eternally polluted by disobedience. Obedience to God can be
thought of as inclusive of faith, humility and love toward God.
Disobedience changed the destiny of mankind. When he became
disobedient, mankind could no longer be in the perfect obedience
requiring presence and environment of God. In the book of
Revelation the obedient person that does the commandments of
God is called blessed by God. That person will have the right to eat
of the tree of life. Obedience gives access to the tree of life and
favor of God. Now you too know the basic requirement of God for
you to enter the Garden of Eden.
It is obedience to the cross of Jesus that spans the gap between the
beginning and the end, as by one man's obedience shall many be
made righteous. Jesus restored perfect obedience. He was obedient
even if He had to die for it. God has highly exalted Jesus. Though
He was a Son, yet learned He obedience by the things which He
suffered, and being made perfect He became the author of eternal
salvation unto all them that obey Him. He is called by God a high
priest after the order of the King of Righteousness, Melchisedec.
Obedience will bless you with understanding the fear of the Lord
and you will find the knowledge of God. Wisdom from God,
knowledge and understanding, protection, and security in God will
be yours as your life will be preserved. Obedience will make you
blameless before God, harmless unto men and the sons of God.
Now consider, who will rebuke you even as you shine as lights,
shine as the sun and the moon? Hold forth the Word of Life as
lighthouses to guide people safely to the harbor of rest. You and
your ways will prosper as you have good success. God will be with
you wherever you go. So be strong and of good courage. Observe
to do all the law as you do not turn left or right from it, nor does
the book of the law depart out of your mouth. Remember that law
is written on the table of your heart. Meditate on it day and night.
Be neither afraid nor dismayed. Pass over your Jordan, that big

river that looks like an obstacle, and possess nations greater than you can even think. God will be with you as a consuming fire to destroy your enemies before you. Drive them out quickly because those nations are wicked. Be not a stiff-necked people. Do not provoke God to wrath and do not be rebellious against Him. Serve none other god.

Love the Lord your God. Keep His charges, statutes, judgments and commandments always, and lay up the words of God in your hearts. Teach them to your children when you sit in your house, or walk by the way, lie down and rise up. Write them upon the door posts of your house and upon your gates. Observe all my statutes and judgments which I set before you this day. Confess your sins. God will hear and forgive your sins confessed, and teach you the good way wherein you should walk. God will bless you with material blessings, answer your prayers, reward you according to your works even as you learn to fear God and know His name. Understand the Power of His Name! God will maintain your cause of loving Him first and above all, love for yourself, and equal love for your neighbor. You will be shown mercy to, by men. Be then obedient to the teachings and word of God as He commands you.

55   The blessings and gifts of Obedience

By obedience to God's Word and diligent study of the Word of God a person is enabled to understand the fear of the Lord and acquire knowledge of God.

How would obedience help us to understand the fear of the Lord? In Proverbs 2:5 Solomon explains to his son to receive his words by his own will, or even to be willing to receive his words. A wise man like Solomon teaches wisdom. Here the wise father teaches his son wisdom. Follow this example. To be taught wisdom so that it would be taken and remembered relates to knowledge of the information that was taught. You must have the desire and unction to achieve knowledge and remember it. Knowledge could be applied or not. If knowledge is understood and wisely applied, that could be thought of as wisdom, coming from Solomon. I hope that the sons of Solomon hid their father's words inside. When wisdom is readily available and also applied, it aims to focus a person on wise things.

WISDOM NEEDS TO BE SO DEEPLY SEATED AS EVEN IN THE HEART OF A PERSON.

* The perfect place to apply wisdom is to your heart.
* Cry for knowledge and lift up your voice for understanding as that is a treasure…,
* But, remember, the fear of the Lord is the beginning of, and all wisdom.
* Seek then the Lord with all your heart.
* The Lord gives wisdom.
* Out of His mouth comes knowledge and understanding.
* He lays up sound wisdom for the righteous.
* He is the buckler to them that walk uprightly.
* What about the Saints? He keeps their paths and preserves their ways!
* How do we find the knowledge of God?
*You are left a choice to seek or not to seek. If you do seek God diligently, you will find Him.
* What makes it by any means important to find the knowledge of God? I would make every effort to understand Joshua 1:8.
* This book of the law shall not depart out of your mouth.
*Thou shall meditate therein day and night.
*Observe to do according to all that is written therein.

*Then thou shall make your way prosperous and be prosperous.

* Be obedient. To enter Paradise, God requires obedience!

*Then we will find wisdom for the Lord gives wisdom.

* Accept that all wisdom, knowledge and understanding come from God.

* When wisdom enters into your heart, knowledge is pleasant unto your soul.

* Discretion shall preserve you.

*Even as understanding shall keep you.

* Pray now and receive from God this security that stays in you.

*You can pull out a checklist and you will find that there is no sin in obedience to the voice of God.

* You cannot fall into temptation if the Lord Jesus is in you.

*Jesus allows no demon or devil in your heart if you make Jesus the Messiah and the King of your heart.

*That is true to scripture and you must not doubt it.

* Obedience to God makes you blameless before God, harmless to men and the sons and daughters of God.

* Nobody can rebuke you!

*Look out, for you will prosper wherever you go.

*Your ways are prosperous and you have good success.

* God will be with you wherever you go as He was with Joshua, so be not afraid or dismayed.

56   <u>COMMANDS OF OBEDIENCE</u>

In warfare, any command by a senior officer must be obeyed. He is respected and obeyed. There is a life of obedience required of the child of God. Statutes and Judgments must be learned, kept and done. If God speaks to man face to face in the midst of fire, most get very afraid. Many were thankful that Moses had to face the presence of God to get what is now written for us in Deuteronomy 4 and contains the orders commanded by God. Let us face it, receiving orders from the Eternal All Star Commander In Chief, scared the Israelites prostrate, face down, physically and emotionally exhausted.

What then are these commandments?

I read this chapter intensely so that I might understand why more than two million people reacted like that.

* 1. A new generation of Hebrews is warned to hear and obey the law. They are asked to hear intelligently and be obedient to the statutes and unto the judgments brought by Moses from God, that they may live, and go in and possess the land which the Lord God gave the Hebrew people.

* 2. No additions or subtractions to the commands were allowed so that they could keep the commandments of the Lord.

* 3. They had to keep to the statutes and judgments of the Lord as this is their wisdom and understanding in the sight of all nations.

* 4.They had to take heed of themselves, and keep their souls diligently, lest they forget what they have seen and their heart depart from them.

* 5. They had to teach these things to their sons and coming generations, that they may learn to fear the Lord all their days.

* 6.The Law required them to take good heed of themselves, lest they corrupt themselves by making graven images, and lest they worship the heavenly bodies like the heathen.

* 7. They had to take heed to themselves lest they forget the covenant of the Lord and make false gods and be consumed by the jealousy of God.

* 8 The Hebrew nation had to know this day and consider in their heart that Jehovah is God.

*. 9. They had to keep His statutes and commandments. Then it

may be well with them and to live long lives.

There were twenty one blessings held before the people of Israel to be obedient to these commands. These were no minor blessings, and one could see how people would want to keep them. The Law was certainly righteous and could govern the actions of the lawless, but it soon became obvious that no man could be blameless. All have sinned and failed to achieve the righteousness that is required by God Almighty. The result of animal sacrifices gave only temporal prosperity, longevity and victory in wars....

How does this differ from the promises of the gospel of Jesus the Messiah?

Is the law made for a righteous man?

Is the law made for the lawless, disobedient, ungodly sinners?

Is the law made for the unholy and profane or murderers of fathers and mothers, manslayers or whoremongers?

Is the law for men stealers, liars or things contrary to sound doctrine?

The law is for people who need their actions governed.

Jesus Christ fulfilled the law and gives us the blessed Holy Spirit to govern us from our hearts.

Internal control by God is the new intimate relational control between Almighty God and blood saved, redeemed, righteous me, all by grace and the sacrifice of the perfect offering: Jesus.

This internal control by Holy Spirit in you is also available to you. Come and walk in that freedom.

57   The Promises of the Gospel

What do we mean by the term GOSPEL?
The first four books of the New Testament are called gospel books.
A part of these are read on a regular basis in churches all over the
world. It is the record of Christ's life on earth, redemption
preached by Christ, the content of His preaching, the spread of the
gospel, anything that is to be firmly believed by the followers of
Christ and is the principle that we should act upon. It is the gospel
of the efficiency and sufficiency of Christ Jesus. Songs are written
to praise Jesus, called gospel songs and sung by slave and freeman.
The Gospel is about the Kingdom of God, and King Jesus. It is
about the Kingdom of the Almighty and how you could become
part of it by the process of salvation from a dead end. There are
written books about this Kingdom affecting billions of people. The
intriguing story of truth has fascinated people over centuries and
continues.... The onset of it starts so long ago as;'' forever and
ever and is about a longer than forever and ever plus evermore to
come, concept, that just keeps on and on continuing...and I have
not been able to really accurately describe the vastness of the Love
of JESUS that the gospel is all about...
A gospel is truth in the most pure definition, incorruptible and
witnessed to the truthfulness of it, multiplied by four books of
witnesses in writing. Written testimonies of power and miracles
and currently believed and agreed on by more than two billion
people over the earth. People that further are prepared to testify' IT
IS AS WITNESSED AND MUCH MORE'!
If I only could describe in real terms what this truth, the power of
the truth and that beauty of it is, and does, I would be doing
billions the greatest favor ever! The Gospel is multiplied by the
Almighty God, Himself. This offer of eternal Live to all would be
noted and accepted, thereby giving His infinite love and grace to
all that would accept it. By far the greatest value that I had ever
represented is simply, that my Lord died for your and my
transgressions and He is still continuing working on every person
that ever missed a goal or mark to accept this grace coming from
the Creator of all. Plainly true! Read the Gospels and be
CONVINCED by God the Holy Spirit as He teaches, about the
gospel of Jesus, the Saviour and Son, sent to come to earth for the

greatest of all missions ever, your and my salvation and invitation to eternal Life with God the Redeemer.

The Gospel is about good news of various kinds, described for you to whosoever believes and accepts the power working Word of God. He works grace in your heart to have faith to believe and thus become washed and cleansed and never to miss this mark again. The real truth is; God is our creator. YOU HAVE BEEN CREATED BY HIM FOR HIM. Accept that and start the new Life of the Gospel as a greatly favored child of God. You will have the blessings of obedience in the power of the grace of God to be strong. You would have rains in due season, abundant crops, days of Heaven on earth, complete mastery of enemies and success in all places. No one would be able to defeat you for the fear in the hearts of your enemies and you would have blessings from God for your obedience to the gospel of God's Word. Check Deuteronomy11, as well as the new testimonies of Matthew, Mark, Luke and John in the Word or Book called the Bible.

Obedience to GOD forms the basis. Believe the Gospel and you will be saved to enter into the Kingdom of God by the cross death of Jesus and His blood spilled for your missing this well-known mark of mankind.

There is only one gospel applicable to Jewish and gentile people and is found declared in the Bible from Matthew to Revelation. It is built on the knowledge of the entire Bible from Genesis to Revelation and not a jot or title is allowed to be changed. I challenge you to disprove the Bible, after you have thoroughly studied and meditated on it day and night, in and out of season as God requires.

The GOSPEL OF THE KINGDOM IS FOR SALVATION AND ALL BENEFITS OF THE GOOD NEWS OF CHRIST. Do you know all the benefits of this gospel?

Go and check it out. You know what to do!

58   Benefits of the Good News of Christ

The initial blessing of the New Covenant is the pardon of sin. God
says it clearly in Hebrews 8: 12-13
I will be merciful to their iniquities. And their sins will I remember
no more. He said that he gave a new covenant. He has made the
first old. But that which is becoming old and waxed aged is nigh
unto vanishing away. The Good News is simple and clear: O
scared and lost sinner, God knows how you cry and suffer because
of the knowledge of your sin. God sees your tears and knows your
agonizing memories. You asked those haunting questions. Why?
Why did I? If only I did not say yes. I should have known! My
child would have been living today…. Tormented and tearing,
your soul cries: Why?
God can help. He pardons. He cares and by His mercy and grace
He has a plan how to turn your problem around. He is prepared to
renew your heart and give you close friendship and fellowship
with Him. Pardon is that entrance, door, or way to get into His
presence. Just pull yourself together enough and take a deep
breath. Now say to Him I am so sorry. Lord, I am really sorry…
Give yourself some time with Him. Even if these awful and ugly
things are the worst things ever done wrong, He is loving and kind
and knows you as you are. Just as you are He still loves you. Even
the worst thing ever done on earth He has forgiven. I BET YOU
FELT LIKE A PERSON WITH SPOTS ALL OVER LIKE
MEASLES OR SCARLET FEVER. Still God loves you and He
now declares you are healed, cleaned, washed and also, He makes
the bold statement that in future He will help you on a new road
that you would know that is just right. This road leads you to
seeking His presence. Wow, that is just something different than
you ever experienced. Can you imagine, the Creator God that
made the world, really wants to dry off those tears and replace it
with His special attention and care and joy all for you... You will
laugh again. The load will lift, that smile is back, and you can face
life again. Now continue and say thank you even as you accept the
present from God. All that I have just explained is what the Son of
God did for us on the cross. He took the punishment for all the

wrong that you had done. He actually was sentence to death for
that. They whipped Him and crucified Him. They gave Him a
crown of thorns and mocked Him. But He carried it all so that you
can reach the target that He has for your life. Ask and consider the
missing of your target as completely forgiven. The very thought of
your sins was thus wiped out of the heart of GOD. Now stand firm
and sin no more. Put away all that you know that is wrong. Do no
wrong anymore. Take up His book, and familiarize yourself with
His teachings and you will be as free as an eagle to fly high. Now
you can glorify God and you will be glad. Surely you will
acknowledge the greatness of God, as He has given your gift of
forgiveness free. Moreover, He will guide, and guard you in a life
of Godliness and growth in wisdom and generosity. Guess what,
you will be a new creation. I mean that the forgiveness of your sins
is so complete that God remembers them no more... Your heart is
now so new that He would write in it the very laws that He wants
you to live by. He will give His Holy Spirit to live inside you to
direct your ways. Holy Spirit wants to be your very best friend. Al
of this is because Jesus was willing to die on the cross for you.
Seek knowledge, believe in Jesus and surrender. That will bring
understanding and acceptance so that you will experience close
fellowship with God, right in His presence and be allowed to stay
there and walk and talk with GOD. Please continue. Surrender
your life as God will be merciful to you and direct your
conscience.
Pardoned! Set free! A new beginning the old life is forever past.
This is not just acquittal, but acceptance and complete restoration
to the heart, love and favor of God.
If God has forgotten your sin, it is gone.

59   FAVOUR

Your grace is enough for me.
Seek first the kingdom of God, and His righteousness, then all
these things shall be added unto you. Lay yourself down at Jesus'
feet and wait upon the Lord only. Take the time you need. It is in
the hands of God by His grace. Honor God. I ask forgiveness for
my arrogance of dishonor, as, even for me to honor God cannot be
but by God's grace.....
Lord, may I please honor you even when there is no human to see
that? What is honor and how far must I go, and what must I do to
honor you, God? Honor is seated in personal integrity. Talking
about seeking Your Kingdom, I tried but got so lost. I can only
laugh at myself. I would love you   please teach me how to
respect and seek God, and as you say, to find righteousness?
The Lord is a God of knowledge. Daddy I need knowledge and
understanding so that my actions could be weighed and pass your
standard. OK I know you tested me and I was brought low, but I
also know that you also lift people up. O Abba, FATHER, please
pick up this poor man out of the dust. Lift this beggar from the
dunghill to set me among princes and make me inherit your love,
for the pillars of the earth are the Lord's and He has set the world
upon them. I do not want to refuse your commands as they are the
principles of all wisdom. Lord teaches me to be wise to honor You,
Jehovah Sabaoth, who formed the mountains, and created the
wind. You declared to man what your thoughts are. You make the
dawn into darkness, and treads on the high places of the earth. You
are the Lord God of Hosts; Jehovah- Sabaoth is Your Name. Is that
You Lord that I serve? Wow!
Then I was guided to the book of Joshua 5:14 and 15 ...What says
my Lord unto His servant? And the captain of the Lord's host said
unto Joshua, Loose your shoe from off your foot; for the place
whereon you stand is HOLY. Holy is your presence even here
now.
It dawned unto me that Joshua had to take the shoes of his feet, just

as Moses had to at the burning bush. I also realized that I would love to live in the will and blessing, grace and favor of the Lord. I want to walk in the presence of the Almighty, talk with Him and worship Him. I really do!

I also had no shoes on my feet as I sensed the Holy presence of God, and realized that the Almighty God is going ahead in His personal victory against Satan and wants me to fight in the battle for souls. So I now know I am prepared. I now know my calling. Come let me run your race as it becomes mine too.

Join me in the prayer of blessing that Jabez asked for.

And Jabez called on the God of Israel saying,
'Oh, that you would bless me indeed,
And enlarge my territory,
That your hand would be with me,
And that you would keep me from evil,
That I may not cause pain! '

So God granted him what he requested. 1 Chronicles 4: 10
Thank you Lord. Thank you. Thanks...
I am blessed indeed.

60   Extraordinary Favor

Lord please gives me 1 Chronicles 4:10 as you gave it to Jabez. I
want to be more honorable, be more and do more for you, precious
Jesus all to the honor of Abba-Father. Let me pray your Word
every day, in humble submission, praise and worship. I call in the
Name of Jesus, to the God of Israel and come to the throne of the
Almighty in awe and adoration. Worthy is Your Name. Holy,
Holy, Holy are You Lord God ALMIGHTY.
By the cross and His life and love and death Jesus met all your
requirements to punish my sins, gracious Father. As I am
reminded, tears well up into my eyes and I worship you. He cried
to You, Father to forgive us as we do not know what we are doing.
I crucified my Jesus. Oh No! I did crucify Him …
You turned it around when I turned away from sin and stood on the
promises of the Word. Your death made all the difference. You lift
me up; you cleaned me up, and dressed me up in new attire. You
gave me your Spirit. I am filled with joy. Those made me do your
will. I ask in Your Name. I ask whatsoever. I ask in your presence
and in Your Vision. I ask by Your Holy Spirit. I ask for your glory
to work as I witness. I ask for souls to come to you. Grace
overcomes us. Love drives us…love drives me as that is who and
what you are: LOVE INDESCRIBABLE. Extend Your Right
Hand of Extraordinary Favor, Love, Grace and Mercy so that I can
live, walks and show your image and do your will. Would that not
enlarge my territory beyond all recognition?
Is that not YOUR FAVOUR TO INTERCEDE FOR BELOVED
PEOPLE? Sinners you know by name, by their body and the hairs
are counted on their head? You know us as we walk and talk and
breathe. IT IS FAVOUR THAT MADE you to appear to Abraham
and Sarah as they sat in the tent door, in the heat of the day in the
plains of Mamre. Favor made you not to pass on from your
servant.
You are the all sufficient God and you are gracious to allow a

mortal to bring water to wash your feet and take time in your schedule. You allowed us the honor to bring unto You a morsel of bread, butter, milk and a love offer of meat to comfort Your Father's heart. I praise your loving kindness to even allow us to run and prepare our best for you. It is but from the very best of a sinner's heart, filthy rags, but what else are worthy? I have nothing worthy to win your favor.

Thank you for wiping away my tears and for your wonderful fellowship and presence just as you had with Abraham and Sarah. You disregard the age and bodily degeneration that we have, even as we offer you obedience, respect and fear and honor and intercession for our brothers and neighbors in need.

Allow us to worship the everlasting God, who is worthy of all the honor and glory that we could give in all eternity. We worship You Lord in the purity of your blood, in the sacrifice of the cross, in the grace of your love, in the power of Your Spirit for eternity... life without end....

61   The Lord Has Blessed Me for Thy Sake

Are you a blessing for someone other than for your own sake? Are you providing only for the sake of someone else and never see any benefit coming to your own family? So was it with Jacob working for his father in law Laban in order to pay for his two wives? The favor of the Lord and His blessings was upon Jacob. Laban scored and he knew it was all because of someone that works for him. That person is diligent, looks after all the affairs with complete passion, and no stone is left in the way to block financial progress and increase. Jacob was the cause of unilateral increase of wealth for his father in law. Even after telling his father in law, Laban still insisted that Jacob should work for him, because he has learned by experience that the Lord has blessed him for the sake of Jacob. Gen 30:27 similarly other people in the Bible were blessed because of some Godly person. Abimelech saw God with Isaac; Potiphar, the jailer, and the Egyptians saw God was with Joseph. Israel saw God with Solomon. Saul saw God with David. Can people see God with you? What does the phrase mean? Do the people see the mercy of God in your life? Do you radiate the favor and share the blessings or even tell people about the blessings of God on your life. If everything you touch prospers, wake up to the blessing of the Almighty God in your life! It is God that gives you blessings to prosper in health. He gives you your talents. Surely thank Him and praise Him, for the Lord is good. You experience it, so tell others and give God the honor.
Just consider yourself special when God say you belong to Him and make you part of His special jewels, and spares you as his own son or daughter. Because you fear His name, the Sun of righteousness arise with healing in his wings. You shall go forth and grow up as calves of the stall, and because you love God you will be as the sun when it goes forth in his might. Because God knows the way that you take, when He tried you, you will come

out as gold. You are blessed because you delight in the law of the Lord and meditate on it day and night. My soul pants after Thee my God. I am like a green olive tree in the house of God as I trust in the mercy of God for ever and ever. O the righteous shall flourish like the palm tree. He shall grow like a cedar in Lebanon. Those that he planted in the house of the Lord shall flourish in the courts of our God. They shall still bring forth fruit in old age…. And they that are wise shall shine as the brightness of the firmament; and they that turn many to righteousness as the stars for ever and ever.

Wait upon the Lord. Renew your strength and mount up with the wings as eagles. RUN because you won't get weary. God loves you. Trust in the Lord and you will not be moved. You will abide forever because the Lord is around you as the mountains around Jerusalem. My little children, these things I write unto you that you sin not. Stay in contact with our advocate with Holy Spirit, the Father, Jesus Christ the righteous who is the propitiation for our sins and also for the sins of the world. Be the lively stones of God's spiritual house, and holy priesthood, to offer up spiritual sacrifices acceptable to God by Jesus Christ. He is the cornerstone. May now the eternal blessing of God the Father, Jesus the Son, and Holy Spirit abide with us in our victorious lives all to the glory of the Father.

35826832R00074